Charles Lukens Davis, Henry Hobart Bellas

A Brief History of the North Carolina Troops on the Continental Establishment

In the War of the Revolution. With a register of officers of the same

Charles Lukens Davis, Henry Hobart Bellas

A Brief History of the North Carolina Troops on the Continental Establishment
In the War of the Revolution. With a register of officers of the same

ISBN/EAN: 9783337115661

Printed in Europe, USA, Canada, Australia, Japan

Cover: Foto ©ninafisch / pixelio.de

More available books at **www.hansebooks.com**

BENJAMIN HAWKINS.

1754–1816.

A BRIEF HISTORY

OF THE

NORTH CAROLINA TROOPS

ON THE

CONTINENTAL ESTABLISHMENT

IN THE WAR OF THE REVOLUTION,

WITH A REGISTER OF OFFICERS OF THE SAME.

BY

CHARLES L. DAVIS,

CAPTAIN TENTH INFANTRY, BREVET MAJOR U. S. ARMY,

Member of Pennsylvania Historical Society; Professor of Military Science, Bingham School, Asheville, North Carolina.

ALSO

A SKETCH

OF THE

NORTH CAROLINA SOCIETY

OF THE

CINCINNATI

FROM ITS ORGANIZATION IN 1783 TO ITS SO-CALLED DISSOLUTION AFTER 1790.

BY

HENRY HOBART BELLAS, LL.B.,

CAPTAIN U. S. ARMY,

Member of Pennsylvania Historical Society; Honorary Member of Delaware and New Hampshire Historical Societies, etc.

PHILADELPHIA, PA.
1896.

CONTENTS.

	PAGE
History of the North Carolina Troops of the Continental Army	3
Register of North Carolina Officers of the Continental Army	34
Preface to Sketch of the North Carolina Society of the Cincinnati	77
Sketch of the North Carolina Society of the Cincinnati	79

A HISTORY

OF THE

North Carolina Troops of the Continental Army,

WITH

A REGISTER OF OFFICERS OF THE SAME.

By CHARLES L. DAVIS,
CAPTAIN TENTH INFANTRY, BREVET MAJOR U.S. ARMY.

REMONSTRANCES and petitions being of no avail with the British Crown, the people of North Carolina, in defence of their rights and liberties, in common with the other colonies, early in 1774, had taken measures to resist the oppressions of their mother-country. William Hooper, writing April 26, 1774, to James Iredell, says, "With you I anticipate the important share which the colonies must soon have in regulating the political balance. They are fast striding to independence, and will ere long build an empire on the ruins of Britain." Safety committees were formed in most of the counties, and, notwithstanding the opposition of the Royal Governor, Josiah Martin, a Provincial Congress met at New Bern, August 25, 1774, of which Colonel John Harvey was elected Moderator, and among its members were the eloquent and polished William Hooper and fiery John Ashe, both from New Hanover, and the proud and wealthy Samuel Johnston, with Joseph Hewes and Thomas Jones, of Chowan, and Robert Howe, of Brunswick (who was afterwards to acquire great military fame), together with many other honorable and patriotic men. This Congress at once appointed delegates (William Hooper, Joseph Hewes, and Richard Caswell) to the Continental Congress, to meet at Philadelphia in the ensuing month of September, and, having passed resolutions expressive of the rights of the colonies, it adjourned November 1, 1774.

The first Continental Congress, meeting at Philadelphia on September 5, 1774, prepared an address to King George III., and passed a resolution to cease all commercial intercourse with Great Britain in case of his refusal to redress the grievances of the colonies. It adjourned October 26, 1774, to meet again May 10, 1775.

Upon the call of Colonel John Harvey, and, notwithstanding the strong opposition of the Royal Governor Martin, another Provincial Congress met at New Bern, April 3, 1775, and, as an indication of the approaching struggle shown in the selection of delegates, they were, in almost every instance, those who were members of the House of Assembly under the Royal authority, and Colonel Harvey was elected the Moderator of one body and Speaker of the other; both bodies sitting at the same time and place, at one time performing the functions of one and then of the other body.

The House of Assembly was dissolved by Governor Martin on April 8, 1775, and stern John Harvey, as Speaker of that body, received the last address which the Royal Governor was to make to it, the last Royal Legislature that met in North Carolina. Without formal dissolution, it at once, with additional members, continued its functions as the Provincial Congress, and returned the same delegates to the Continental Congress to meet in Philadelphia in May, 1775. Governor Martin called his Council together and denounced the acts of the Provincial Congress. For defence he caused a few guns to be placed before his palace at New Bern; but, while he and his Council were in session, these guns were seized by a body of brave men, headed by Dr. Alexander Gaston and Richard Cogdell, on April 24, 1775, and carried away. The terrified Governor, with a few followers, fled at once to Wilmington, and thence, soon afterwards, to Fort Johnson, at the mouth of Cape Fear River, from which he was driven on July 15, 1775, by Colonels James Moore and John Ashe,* with a body of troops, to

---

* Colonel John Ashe was born 1721. His father, John Baptista Ashe, the founder of the family, emigrated from England in the early part of 1727. He was a friend of Lord Craven, under whose patronage he came, with his family, to seek his fortune in the Western world. He was a gentleman of liberal education, accomplished manners, and superior intellect, and in 1730 was one of the Council of Governor George Burrington, of North Carolina. His two sons, John and Samuel, as well as their sons, were distinguished in the field of battle and councils of the State. Of this family there were in the Revolutionary War seven officers—Brigadier-General John Ashe, of the militia from the District of Wilmington, with his sons, Captains John and Samuel of the Continental Army (the latter of whom was a member of the North Carolina Society of the Cincinnati); Paymaster Samuel Ashe, Sr., with his sons, Lieutenant-Colonel John Baptista Ashe and Lieutenant Samuel Ashe, Jr., of the Continentals and Captain Cincinnatus Ashe, of the Marines, the latter of whom was lost at sea. Lieutenant-Colonel J. B. Ashe was a member of the North Carolina Society of the Cincinnati, a member of the Continental Congress in 1787–8, and from 1790 to 1793 a member of the Congress under the Constitution. In 1795 he represented Halifax in the House of Commons of North Carolina, and was afterwards elected Governor of the State, but died

take refuge on board the Royal warship Cruizer, whence he continued to fulminate proclamations forbidding the forming of a provincial council of delegates from the counties.

In April, 1775, the British Parliament, in order to punish the colonies, had passed an act restraining the American colonies from trade and commerce with Great Britain and the West Indies, excepting in its provisions the colonies of New York, Georgia, and North Carolina. North Carolina, regarding this as an effort to seduce its people to desert the common cause, refused to accept this advantage, and continued to adhere to the plans of the Continental Congress. The weight of this obnoxious law was falling only on the city of Boston, Massachusetts, which was held by General Gage in a state of siege. At length, on the 19th of April, 1775, came the affair of Lexington and Concord, Massachusetts. News travelled slowly in those days, and it was not until May 19 that the intelligence of this bloodshed was received at the village of Charlotte, in Mecklenburg, North Carolina. The patriot sons of Mecklenburg County, composed of two representatives from each militia company, as delegates to a county committee, in session at Charlotte,

---

November 27, 1802, before inauguration. His grandson, John Jefferson Ashe, is now a distinguished citizen of Tipton County, Tennessee. Of the descendants of Lieutenant Samuel Ashe, Jr., who was the last surviving officer of the North Carolina Continentals, there are many distinguished persons throughout the country. His eldest son, John Baptista Ashe, was a member of Congress from Tennessee and has a son, Captain Samuel S. Ashe, a distinguished citizen of Houston, Texas. A grandson of Lieutenant Samuel Ashe, Captain Samuel A. Ashe, is now a prominent lawyer and journalist of Raleigh, North Carolina. Lieutenant Samuel Ashe died in the latter part of 1835.

SAMUEL ASHE, Jr.

1763–1835.

received the news of this act of violence with horror, and, though far from the scene of bloodshed, they felt that the cause of New England was theirs too.

The famous Mecklenburg Declaration of Independence was resolved the next day, May 20, 1775, to the maintenance of which they solemnly pledged their lives fortunes, and most sacred honor. These resolutions were drafted by Dr. Ephraim Brevard, and signed as follows:

Abraham Alexander,	John McKnitt Alexander,
Chairman.	*Secretary.*
Ephraim Brevard.	Matthew McClure.
Hezekiah J. Balch.	Ezra Alexander.
James Harris.	John Flennikin.
Waightstill Avery.	Richard Harris, Sr.
Richard Barry.	Thomas Polk.
Neil Morrison.	Adam Alexander.
William Graham.	Charles Alexander.
David Reese.	William Kennon.
Hezekiah Alexander.	Benjamin Patton.
John Phifer.	Henry Downs.
Zacheus Wilson, Sr.	Robert Irwin.
John Ford.	John Queary.

Copies of these resolutions were sent to the Provincial Congress and to the Continental Congress, but it is believed were never presented to the latter body, as the act was regarded as premature, for the colonies were not yet convinced that reconciliation was impossible. The American colonies having been declared in Parliament to be in a state of actual rebellion, it was conceived, in connection with the Mecklenburg Declaration of Independence, that all laws and commissions from Royal authority, so far as Mecklenburg County was concerned, were annulled by these resolutions, and the county committee in session at Charlotte provided for the exigency by a series of twenty resolutions, dated May 31, 1775, providing for the government and protection of their county. Thus the county of Mecklenburg, North Carolina, by these bold acts, was the first region to absolutely dissolve the bonds of allegiance which had so long connected them with the British Crown.

The Continental Congress met, according to adjournment, in Philadelphia, May 10, 1775, and June 15, 1775, saw Washington appointed Commander-in-Chief of the American forces. A Provincial Congress was called to meet at Hillsboro, North Carolina, against the meeting of which Governor Martin, from the deck of the British war-vessel Cruizer, issued proclamations. They met, nevertheless, at Hillsboro, August 21, 1775, and elected Samuel Johnston, of Chowan, as President. The die was cast, and North Carolina was at last a self-governing commonwealth, with the people united in opposition to Great Britain, and they proceeded to arm for battle.

Militia companies had been organized in some of the counties as early as 1774. Before March 10, 1775, a regiment had been organized in Brunswick and Hanover Counties under Colonel Robert Howe. Colonel John Ashe had given up a commission under the Royal Governor

Martin and appeared in Wilmington early in 1775 with four or five hundred armed men. In Mecklenburg County the militia had been organized under authority of the resolutions of the County Committee of May 31, 1775. The regiment under Colonel Howe will hereafter appear as part of the troops organized for Continental service.

The Congress at Hillsboro declared that North Carolina was bound by the acts of the Continental Congress, and would support its decrees to the extent of all its power, and it was resolved that North Carolina would pay a proper proportion of the burden incurred in support of a Continental army. A Provincial Council, composed of twelve men, was created by this Congress, which was to execute the power of the colony, at the head of which was placed Cornelius Harnett, of New Hanover. Six battalions of minute-men were authorized, the county militia were enrolled and drilled, to be under the control of the Provincial Council, and, in addition to these, two regiments of Continental troops were enlisted for the war,—the first under Colonel James Moore, and the second under Colonel Robert Howe.

The Congress at Hillsboro adjourned September 10, 1775, and in less than sixty days thereafter Colonel Howe, with his regiment of Continentals and a battalion of militia under Colonel Benjamin Wynns, was near Norfolk, Virginia, defending that State against Lord Dunmore.

The appreciation of his services in Virginia is shown by the following resolution of the Virginia Convention in session at Williamsburg, December 22, 1775:

"*Resolved unanimously*, That the thanks of this Convention are justly due to the brave officers, gentlemen volunteers and soldiers of North Carolina, as well as our brethren of that province in general, for their prompt and generous aid in defence of our common rights against the enemies of America and of the British Constitution; and that the President be desired to transmit a copy of this resolution to Colonel Howe."

It will be seen from this that North Carolina was probably the first to send troops beyond her borders for common defence against the oppressions of Great Britain. Nor was this all, for, about the same time that Colonel Howe moved towards Norfolk, an important expedition, composed of militia, was organized in Western North Carolina, under Colonels Griffith Rutherford, of Rowan, Thomas Polk, of Mecklenburg, and James Martin, of Guilford, to assist General Richardson and Colonel Thompson, commanding the South Carolina Whig forces, in suppression of a rising of certain royalists, called "Scovilites," at Ninety Six, in South Carolina.

In the autumn of 1775, upon the suggestion of Governor Martin, a vigorous campaign against the colonies was attempted by Sir Henry Clinton. As to North Carolina, it was expected there would be a strong co-operation by the Scotch and "Regulators," royalists who were expected to assemble in the upper region of the Cape Fear Valley under a General Donald McDonald of His Majesty's forces. A short and brilliant campaign of a month, under Colonel James Moore, of the First North Carolina Continentals, assisted by the militia under Colonels Caswell and Lillington and Captain J. B. Ashe, resulted in a battle at Moore's Creek, February 27, 1776, with a complete destruction of the forces under McDonald, and prevented the junction of Clinton with the Scotch and Regulators. The Provincial

OF THE CONTINENTAL ARMY.

Council, then in session at New Bern, in recognition of the services of Colonel Moore in this short campaign, and of Colonel Howe in the colony of Virginia, passed the following resolutions, March 4, 1776:

"*Resolved*, That the thanks of this Council be given to Colonel James Moore * and all the brave officers and soldiers of every denomination for their late very important services rendered their country in effectually suppressing the late daring and dangerous insurrection of the Highlanders and Regulators, and that this Resolve be published in the *North Carolina Gazette*.

"*Resolved*, That Colonel Robert Howe is justly entitled to the most honorable testimony of the approbation of this Council for his important services while in the Colony of Virginia, rendered in the common cause of American liberty, and that the President transmit the warmest thanks of this Board, in the fullest and most honorable terms, to Colonel Howe and all the brave officers and soldiers under his command for their spirited conduct, having acquitted themselves greatly to their honor and the good of their country."

Colonels Robert Howe and James Moore were appointed Brigadier-Generals in the Continental Army, March 1, 1776. Howe became a Major-General, October 20, 1777; served to

---

* General James Moore was born in New Hanover, North Carolina, in 1737, and died in Wilmington, North Carolina, January 15, 1777. He was the son of Captain Maurice Moore, of Charleston, South Carolina, and grandson of Governor James Moore, of the latter colony, who subsequently became attorney-general, judge of the admiralty court, and Speaker of the South Carolina Assembly. Governor Moore was himself the son of Colonel James Moore, also Governor of South Carolina, 1719, and brother of Honorable John Moore, Esquire, one of the most prominent and aristocratic men of the province of Pennsylvania, and the head of the Moore family of that State, as well as of New York and Virginia.

Descended from Rory o'Moore a celebrated Irish Chieftain

the close of the war; was a member of the North Carolina Society of the Cincinnati, and died November 12, 1785. General Moore died January 15, 1777.

On the 4th of April, 1776, the Provincial Congress again met at Halifax, and on April 12, 1776, unanimously passed a resolution empowering the North Carolina delegates in the Continental Congress to concur with the delegates of the other colonies in declaring independence; and thus, with Sir Henry Clinton and his forces still floating in the waters on her coast, North Carolina was in advance of all the colonies in proclaiming to the world her determination to be free and independent of the British Crown. North Carolina, with just pride, bears this date, as well as that of the Mecklenburg Declaration of Independence (May 20, 1775), upon her State flag.

On April 13, 1776, this Congress ordered four additional Continental regiments to be raised, the officers of which were appointed on the 15th and 16th, and "arranged to regiments" on the 17th. Three troops of Light Horse had also been ordered by the same Congress on April 9.

By a letter from Joseph Hewes, delegate to the Continental Congress, dated Philadelphia, May 16, 1776, to Samuel Johnston, President of the Provincial Congress, it appears that the six regiments were accepted by the Continental Congress, and the appointment of Colonel Nicholas Long to be Deputy Quartermaster-General was confirmed, but that the troops of Light Horse were not then accepted, though they appear to have been at a later period, for some of the officers deranged by the rearrangement of June 1, 1778, were transferred to the Light Horse.

General Charles Lee, of Virginia, who had been appointed a Major-General as early as June 17, 1775, had been assigned to the command of the Southern forces. On June 1, 1776, the fleet of Sir Henry Clinton, to which there had been joined the command of Lord Cornwallis, left the mouth of Cape Fear River and sailed for Charleston, South Carolina. The first and second regiments, under command of General Moore, were hurried off to Charleston, where they arrived June 11. On June 28, the British fleet under Sir Peter Parker attacked Fort Moultrie on Sullivan's Island, the troops under Cornwallis attempting to land on the island. Colonel Thompson, with the South Carolina Rangers and a battalion of two hundred picked men of the First North Carolina Continentals, under Lieutenant-Colonel Thomas Clark, handsomely repulsed this attempt to land. The gallantry of the North Carolina troops is attested in General Lee's letter to Hon. Edmund Pendleton, of Virginia, under date of June 29, 1776, wherein he says,—

"I know not which corps I have the greatest reason to be pleased with, Muhlenburgh's Virginians or the North Carolina troops. They are both equally alert, zealous, and spirited."

From a letter of Colonel Jethro Sumner, of the Third Regiment, to Lieutenant-Colonel Alston, dated Savannah, Georgia, September 3, 1776, it would appear that his regiment had also been sent South, and that it was not assembled at Wilmington in July and August, as were the other regiments.

The resolution of independence of the colonies was introduced in the Continental Congress, June 7, 1776, and after debate it was passed on July 2, 1776. On July 4, 1776, the formal Declaration of Independence of the thirteen colonies was unanimously adopted by that body, and on August 1, 1776, it was joyously proclaimed at Halifax amid military displays and a vast assemblage of people.

On November 12, 1776, a Congress met at Halifax to form a State Constitution. System was brought out of chaos, and the executive functions were vested in a Governor and an Assembly consisting of two houses. Richard Caswell was elected Governor, and he assumed his duties December 23, 1776, upon the adjournment of the Congress.

Upon the defeat of Sir Peter Parker and Lord Cornwallis at Sullivan's Island, June 28 and 29, 1776, the North Carolina troops soon found no enemy in their presence. In July and August, 1776, the regiments of the North Carolina Line were concentrated at Wilmington, excepting the Third, which probably did not arrive until some weeks later. They were drilled and rigidly disciplined in this camp until about the middle of November, when they were ordered North to re-enforce General Washington's army. On reaching Halifax they were halted for three weeks, and then countermarched to the vicinity of Charleston to meet the British, who were near St. Augustine, Florida, threatening Georgia and South Carolina. At a pause on this journey near the boundary of South Carolina many of them claimed their discharge, and several men deserted, among these being three free colored men. At the urgent request of the authorities of Georgia and South Carolina, these troops were retained for the defence of those States until March 15,

1777, when they were again ordered to join General Washington, who was retreating through New Jersey with great loss and in extreme danger.

The route pursued by these troops was by Wilmington, Halifax, Richmond, Alexandria, and Georgetown, and, as the story of their victorious deeds in the South preceded them, their progress through Virginia and Maryland was an ovation. At Alexandria those who had not suffered with the small-pox were inoculated, with such success that not a man was lost from that disease thereafter. Some of these regiments reached Washington's camp at Middlebrook, New Jersey, about the last of June, 1777; the others joined near Philadelphia soon afterwards. All of them were placed in the command of Major-General William Alexander (Lord Stirling), and there appears to have been some cavalry and artillery from North Carolina with them. The cavalry, consisting of two troops of light horse, was returned to the service of the State, by an order of the Board of War, dated November 24, 1778.

The Congress, assembled at Halifax, November 12, 1776, had, on November 26, 1776, ordered three additional regiments—Seventh, Eighth, and Ninth—to be raised for the Continental establishment; and, as other troops followed from North Carolina to re-enforce Washington's army during the remainder of the year 1777, all these regiments joined that army before the battle of Germantown, and accompanied Washington to his camp at Valley Forge. A tenth regiment was organized in April, 1777, and it appears to have joined Washington after his going into winter camp at Valley Forge.

The arrival of these re-enforcements from the South enabled Washington to resume the aggressive against the British commander, Sir William Howe, who had transferred his troops by water to the Head of Elk, Maryland, with the design of moving on Philadelphia. General Washington met the forces of Howe, September 11, 1777, at Chadd's Ford, on the Brandywine, where he was compelled to fight a battle; and, although Howe won a victory and gained possession of Philadelphia, the success at Brandywine fell to ashes in his hands, for in less than a year his troops were withdrawn from Philadelphia, the possession of which had cost the British the capture of Burgoyne at Saratoga. In the battle of Brandywine, the North Carolina troops found themselves under Stirling's command as part of the right wing and in the command of General Sullivan. It fell to their lot to oppose the flanking movement of Lord Cornwallis, and that the retreat of Stirling's and Stephen's divisions was effected with steadiness and repeated returns to the offensive, notwithstanding the blunders of General Sullivan, is shown by the fact that they were able, in this disastrous affair, to bring off the field their artillery and baggage.

It was, however, at Germantown, October 4, 1777, that the valor of the North Carolina troops was conspicuous. The enemy being weakened by detachments sent against the forts on the Delaware, General Washington seized the opportunity to fall upon him at that place, and was only prevented from complete success by a combination of unfortunate circumstances. Colonel Francis Nash, of the First Regiment, had been promoted to Brigadier-General in

1759–1834.

the Continental Army, February 5, 1777, and he led the brigade of North Carolina troops in this battle. It formed part of the reserve under Major-General Stirling, and was thrown into the attack on the right, where its conduct gained the high encomiums of the Commander-in-Chief.

Of this battle, which ended in a disastrous defeat of our forces, General Washington said, in a letter to the Continental Congress, three days afterwards, as follows:

> "Our troops retreated when victory was declaring in our favor. The tumult, disorder, and even despair which, it is said, had taken place in the British army, were scarcely paralleled."

And a British writer bestows the following compliment upon the American army in this affair:

> "In this action the Americans acted on the offensive, and, though repulsed with loss, showed themselves a formidable adversary, capable of charging with resolution and retreating with order. The hope, therefore, entertained from the effect of any fair action with them, as [*sic*] decisive and likely to put a speedy termination to the war, was exceedingly abated."

Of the North Carolina Continentals there fell on that day, killed on the field, Lieutenant-Colonel Henry Irwin, of the Fifth, and Captain Jacob Turner, of the Third Regiments; mortally wounded, Colonel Edward Buncombe, of the Fifth, who was taken prisoner, and died in captivity at Philadelphia shortly afterwards, and Brigadier-General Francis Nash, who died three days after the battle. Major William Polk, of the Ninth, was also badly wounded. A reliable account of the wounding of General Nash is as follows: While riding down the main street of Germantown, leading the North Carolina brigade into action, a round shot, fired by the British, struck and fractured his thigh, at the same time killing his horse. The fall of the animal threw its rider to the ground with considerable force. Retaining his presence of mind, General Nash, covering his shattered thigh with his hands, called to his men: " Never mind me. I have had a devil of a tumble; rush on, my boys; rush on the enemy; I'll be after you presently." Human nature could do no more. He was borne fainting from the field, faithfully cared for, and after three days of terrible suffering he died, and was buried with military honors in the Mennonist graveyard at Kulpsville, Pennsylvania.

Soon after the serious check at Germantown, General Washington took his army into winter quarters at Valley Forge (December 19, 1777), on the Schuylkill, about twenty miles above Philadelphia. At this distance of time, it is difficult to realize the privations and sufferings of Washington's army in the hutted camp which he established at Valley Forge. They are dimly divulged in his order of March 1, 1778, every line of which breathes patriotism:

"HEAD-QUARTERS, March 1, 1778.

"The Commander-in-Chief again takes occasion to return his warmest thanks to the virtuous officers and soldiers of the army for the fidelity manifested in all their conduct. Their fortitude, not only under the common hardships incidental to military life, but also under the additional sufferings to which the peculiar situation of these states has exposed them, clearly proves them worthy the invaluable privilege of contending for the rights of human nature, the freedom and independence of their country. The recent instance of uncomplaining patience, during the scarcity of provisions in camp, is a fresh proof that they possess the magnanimity of patriots. The few refractory individuals who disgraced themselves by murmurs, it is to be hoped, have repented such unmanly behavior and resolved to emulate the noble example of their associates upon every trial which the customary casualties of war may hereafter throw in their way. Occasionally distress for want of provisions and other necessaries is a spectacle that frequently occurs in every army. There never was one which has, in general, been so plentifully supplied, in respect to the former, as ours. Surely, we, who are free citizens in arms engaged in a struggle for everything valuable in society and partaking in the glorions task of laying the foundation of an empire, should seem effeminate to shrink, under those accidents and rigors of war which mercenary hirelings, fighting in the cause of lawless ambition, rapine, and devastation, encounter with cheerfulness and alacrity. We should not be nearly equal; we should be superior to them in every qualification that dignifies the man or the soldier in proportion as the motives from which we act and the final hopes that our toils are superior to theirs. Thank heaven! our country abounds with provisions, and, with prudent management, we need not apprehend want for any length of time. Defects in the commissary department, contingencies of weather, and other temporary impediments have subjected, and may again subject, us to a deficiency for a few days. But, *soldiers!* AMERICAN SOLDIERS! should be above the meanness of repining at such trifling strokes of adversity; trifling, indeed, are they when compared with the transcendent prize which will undoubtedly crown your patience and perseverance,—glory and freedom, peace and plenty, the admiration of the world, the love of your fellow-countrymen, and the gratitude of posterity will be your reward. Your General incessantly employs his thoughts on the means of relieving your distresses, supplying your wants, and bringing your labors to a speedy and prosperous issue. Our parent country, he hopes, will second his endeavors by the most vigorous execution, and he is convinced the faithful officers and soldiers associated with him in the great work of rescuing our country from bondage and misery will continue in the display of that patriotic zeal which is capable of smoothing every difficulty and vanquishing every obstacle."

The regiments composing the North Carolina brigade at Valley Forge, being greatly reduced by the casualties of war, were, on June 1, 1778, under a resolution of Congress of May 29, 1778, consolidated into four. The Tenth Regiment, then in camp with General Washington, appears to have retained its number, for a report of the camp equipage of the Northern army, made by General Nathaniel Greene, Quartermaster-General, in June, 1778, gives the North Carolina brigade as composed of the First, Second, Third, and Tenth Regiments, under the command of Colonel Thomas Clark, the senior officer on duty with it, for Brigadier-General Lochlan McIntosh, the former commander, had been ordered on other duty May 26, 1778. The subsequent history of the Tenth Regiment is obscure, for it will appear later on that it was not surrendered with the other North Carolina regiments at Charleston, May 12, 1780. It seems to have disappeared to history, excepting in the records of the State, where appointments to it are shown, in each successive year, as late as 1782.

After spending the winter in Philadelphia in gayeties and riotous living, General Howe had been superseded by Lieutenant-General Clinton, and on the 18th of June, 1778, the city was evacuated by the British, who crossed the Delaware below the city, and, encumbered by a huge baggage train, they hoped to reach New York safely.

General Washington crossed the Delaware above Philadelphia and overtook the enemy at Monmouth, New Jersey, June 28, 1778, where, notwithstanding the ill-timed retreat, disobedience, and treachery of General Charles Lee in the early part of the action, General Washington discomfited the British, although he did not prevent their retreat, with all their baggage, to New York.

My studies lead me to think that the North Carolina brigade was in General Stirling's division, forming the left of the second line, which General Washington placed under

General Lafayette, after the ignominious retreat of Lee; but from a "Field Return of the Troops under the immediate command of His Excellency, Genl. Washington," dated June 28, 1778, it seems to appear that there were but two regiments in the North Carolina brigade on the day of that battle. These were, doubtless, the First and Second. Where were the Third and Tenth? The North Carolina troops won high commendation for their conduct on this field of battle. The First and Second North Carolina Regiments took part in all the movements of Lafayette's division from Valley Forge to the Hudson River, and were located at Paramus, New Jersey, in March, 1779, the Third being then in Philadelphia undergoing inoculation. It appears that the First and Second were at West Point, New York, late in 1779, and were the last of the North Carolina Continentals to join General Lincoln in Charleston in the winter of 1779-80.

The sources of information in regard to the North Carolina Continentals during the period of which I write are very meagre, but it is hoped that the forthcoming State Records of North Carolina, compiled and edited by Hon. Walter Clark, in continuation of the series of Colonial Records, together with the publication of the records of the Revolutionary War, now in the War Department at Washington, for which there is reason to believe that provision will soon be made, will tell the story of their sufferings, privations, and gallant conduct.

The most brilliant feat of arms that occurred during the American Revolution was that performed at Stony Point, on the night of July 16, 1779, by a select body of troops under

General Anthony Wayne, in which there were two companies of the Second North Carolina Continentals, led by the gallant Major Hardy Murfree.* Stony Point was a rocky promontory on the west bank of the Hudson, about one hundred and fifty feet high, the occupation of which by the enemy was a menace to West Point and Washington's communications with New England. The attack was made in two columns, the right under Colonel Christian Febiger, of Virginia, and the left under Colonel Richard Butler, of Pennsylvania, with which went Major Murfree's battalion of two companies. They were to advance with absolute silence and unloaded muskets, relying only on the bayonet. When the left column reached a certain point, Major Murfree's battalion was to open a furious fire on the front of the works,

---

* Major Hardy Murfree was born in Hartford County, North Carolina, June 5, 1752, and was the son of William Murfree, a member from that county in the North Carolina Congress that convened at Halifax, November, 1776, and framed the Constitution that, without amendment, continued to be the organic law of the State from 1776 to 1835. The son entered the army at the age of twenty-three and served throughout the war. His brilliant service at the capture of Stony Point is well known. The sword he wore on this occasion is now in the possession of the Tennessee Historical Society, and his descendants retain the blood-stained sash he used in helping to bear General Nash from the battle-field of Germantown. After the war, Major Murfree resided on his plantation on the banks of the Meherrin River, near Murfreesboro', North Carolina. In 1807 he emigrated to Tennessee and settled on Murfree's Fork of West Harpeth, in Williamson County. He died in Williamson County, Tennessee, July 6, 1809. The town of Murfreesboro' was named in his honor. His letters show he was well educated and intelligent. His descendants still reside in the State, one—Mary Noailles Murfree, his great-granddaughter—being quite celebrated as an authoress to-day, under the pen-name of Charles Egbert Craddock.

1748-1804.

in order to draw attention from the flanking columns. The right and left columns were to capture the outposts and, attacking the defenders, force their way over and around the abattis and enter the fort by the sally-port. The watchword, to be given in a shout as they entered the works, was "The fort is ours!"

The columns formed at the foot of the hill, each preceded by one hundred and fifty determined men, twenty of whom were placed in advance as "forlorn hopes," led by two young Pennsylvania lieutenants. The advance guard followed the forlorn hopes. The one on the left was led by Major Stewart, of Maryland; that on the right by Lieutenant-Colonel Fleury, of the Engineers, where General Wayne, in person, directed the column. Major Murfree, being in the centre, between these columns, advanced up the slope. The right column was somewhat delayed by wading through water. Meantime Major Murfree began, as a feint, a tremendous firing of musketry. The forlorn hope of each column rushed forward to its duty, and the columns followed closely, amid a shower of grape-shot and musketry. The right column first entered the fort, led by Colonel Fleury, General Wayne being wounded in the head. So accurately had the movements been timed and the plans and orders been carried out, that both columns, as well as Major Murfree's two companies, reached the interior of the fort almost simultaneously. Among the casualties at Stony Point were Lieutenant William Hilton killed and Lieutenant John Daves wounded, both of Major Murfree's battalion.

General Wayne's laconic despatch, announcing his success, was as follows:

"STONY POINT, 16 July, 2 A.M.
"DEAR GEN'L,
"The fort and garrison with Col. Johnston are ours. Our officers and men behaved like men who are determined to be free.
"Yours most sincerely,
"ANTH'Y WAYNE.
"GENL. WASHINGTON."

In a supplemental report to Congress on this assault, General Wayne writes as follows:

"WEST POINT, August 10th, 1779.
"SIR:
"Your very polite favor of the 17th ult., with the extract of an act of Congress, I have just received. The honorable manner in which that respectable Body have been pleased to express their approbation of my conduct in the enterprise on Stony Point must be very flattering to a young soldier; but, whilst I experience every sensation arising from a consciousness of having used my best endeavors to carry the orders of my General into execution, I feel very much hurt that I did not in my letter of the 17th of July mention (among other brave and worthy officers) the names of Lieut. Col. Sherman, Majors Hull, MURFREE, and Posey, whose good conduct and intrepidity justly entitled them to that attention. Permit me therefore, thro' your Excellency, to do them that justice now which the state of my wound diverted me from in the first instance.

"I am,
"With every sentiment of esteem,
"Your Excellency's most obedient humble servant,
"ANTH'Y WAYNE.
"His Excellency JOHN JAY ESQ.,
"*President of Congress.*"

The officers of the North Carolina Continentals who were deranged by the arrangement of June 1, 1778, were returned to their State, to be assigned to other regiments authorized to be levied there. Some were transferred to State troops, and such as could not be retained were honorably discharged. That many of them continued in service is shown by the fact that, among the casualties, in General Jethro Sumner's brigade at Stone Ferry, June 20, 1779, we find, mortally wounded, Captain James Campbell, formerly of the Second Regiment, and Ensign William Charlton; wounded, Colonel James Armstrong, formerly of the Eighth (commanding at the time North Carolina Rangers), Lieutenant-Colonel Archibald Lytle, formerly of the Sixth, Major Henry Dixon, formerly of the Third, and Captain Joseph T. Rhodes, formerly of the Tenth.

In the last days of 1778 the tide of war turned southward. The plan of the enemy was to subdue Georgia and, sweeping through the Carolinas, to form a junction in Virginia or Maryland with the troops from the northward, thus carrying out the so-called "plan" of the treacherous Charles Lee. On December 29, 1778, Savannah was captured, and Sir Henry Clinton was on his way by water from New York to Charleston with re-enforcements destined to the investment and capture of that place. To General Benjamin Lincoln had been assigned the defence of Charleston, and, in November, 1779, General Washington sent the North Carolina Continentals to re-enforce him. They were under the command of Brigadier-General James Hogun, who, as also Jethro Sumner, had been promoted January 9, 1779; Hogun's promotion being based on his distinguished intrepidity at Germantown. As the North Carolina Continentals passed through Philadelphia from their cantonments on the Hudson, this gallant brigade numbered only about seven hundred men. It was a terrible winter journey for them. The troops suffered greatly, and did not reach Charleston until March 13, 1780. In writing to Lafayette, Washington said of this event as follows,—

"The extreme cold, the deep snows and other impediments, retarded the march of the North Carolina brigade. The oldest people now living do not remember so hard a winter. The severity of the frost exceeded anything of the kind that had ever been experienced in this climate."

Clinton effected a landing on the islands south of Charleston, and, crossing the Stone and Ashley Rivers in the latter part of March, 1780, procceded to lay siege to the city from the land side. The first parallel was completed April 9, and a surrender demanded the next day, which was promptly refused. A bombardment was commenced and kept up almost incessantly until May 9, when a second demand for surrender met with a second refusal. A tremendous cannonade ensued, which ended only when a capitulation took place, May 12, 1780.

The defence of Charleston was undertaken for political rather than military reasons, for it was deemed that the effect of the evacuation of that principal Southern city would prove disastrous to the American cause. Nevertheless, General Lincoln did intend to evacuate, but the tardy plans of General Clinton changed his views, for he had been promised large re-enforcements, one-half to be regulars. He also hoped for re-enforcements from the Spanish West Indies.

With the surrender of Charleston the whole of the North Carolina Continentals became prisoners of war excepting some few officers and men who were then absent from their commands. North Carolina lost fifty-nine officers, belong-

1756–1820.

ing to the First, Second, and Third Regiments and a battery of artillery, nearly all her regulars, and a thousand disciplined militia. At a time when the country could illy spare any of her defenders, the veteran soldiers of the Carolinas, penned in British prison-ships, were perishing of disease and despair; among the victims being the commander of the North Carolina brigade, General James Hogun, who refused a parole that would separate him from his comrades in misfortune and died January 4, 1781, in captivity.

That some of the North Carolina Continentals escaped the disaster at Charleston seems to appear from the names of killed and wounded at Ramsour's Mills, June 20, 1780. Captains —— Dobson and Joshua Bowman were killed and Captain William Armstrong (all of the First) was wounded, while at King's Mountain, October 7, 1780, Captain James Williams was killed and Captain Micajah Lewis (both of the Fourth) wounded.

Although a small force of Maryland, Virginia, and Delaware Continentals remained to defend the Carolinas, these States now largely depended on their militia for protection. The battles of King's Mountain, Cowpens, and Eutaw Springs tell of their valor under skilful leaders.

Soon after the surrender of General Lincoln at Charleston, General Washington sent General Horatio Gates to command the Southern department. He assumed command July 25, 1780. The battle of Camden, fought August 16, 1780, was a disaster, due to his over-confidence, failure to use his cavalry for exploring, and the bad conduct of the militia, but the latter soon retrieved their reputation at King's Mountain. Major-General Nathaniel Greene shortly afterwards (December 3, 1780) followed Gates in command of the South, and the battle of Cowpens, January 17, 1781, illustrated the valor of militia well led. Guilford followed March 15, 1781, and gave a turning-point to the career of Lord Cornwallis, which terminated with his surrender at Yorktown, October 19, 1781.

Shortly after the battle of Guilford, General Greene gave his attention to the re-establishment of the North Carolina Line. There were in the State a few hundred men that had been left behind or had escaped capture at Charleston, and there were also the supernumerary officers who had lost their commands at the reorganization of June 1, 1778. General Jethro Sumner was placed in charge of this matter. In August, 1780, he had been called to the command of the militia at Charlotte, but had withdrawn therefrom when superseded by General Smallwood, and he then renewed his exertions to reorganize his brigade, appealing to the patriotism of the people and exhausting every effort to obtain arms, which he finally obtained from Virginia. The Legislature of North Carolina met at Halifax, January 18, 1781, and, complying with the resolves of the Continental Congress, reduced the number of regiments of the Continentals, required to be furnished by the State, from six to four. Impressment by a draft became necessary, and an act was passed punishing refusal to perform military duty as follows:

"Those persons who have been lawfully drafted and have neglected or refused to march and go into actual service on due notice, or find a substitute, as is therein directed, shall be held and deemed *a Continental soldier for twelve months;* and that those persons who have deserted their colors when in actual service, shall be held and deemed a *Continental soldier during the war."*

General Sumner met the officers then in the State who could convene, at Halifax January 23, 1781, to make an arrangement of the Continental line, but, finding a difficulty in procuring the dates of commissions of those in captivity whose release was soon expected, a temporary arrangement was made.

By a general exchange of prisoners, agreed upon in April, 1781, between General Greene and Lord Cornwallis, many veterans who had been inactive since the fall of Charleston were released. By the arrangement made at Halifax, Colonel John B. Ashe, Major Hardy Murfree, Major Henry Dixon, and John Armstrong were to command the four regiments. Major Pinketham Eaton was at this time with Colonel Lee's Legion in command of a battalion formed from the militia who had fled from the battle of Guilford to their homes, but he was yearning to be of General Sumner's command. He fell gallantly, at the head of his battalion, in the moment of victory, beloved by all that knew him, in the attack on Fort Grierson, one of the defences of Augusta, Georgia, on June 5, 1781. Ninety of his men were subsequently absorbed in the Continentals of General Sumner's brigade.

Honorable David Schenk says of the men under Major Eaton as follows:

"The splendid courage and dash of the command of Eaton, composed, as it was, *entirely of militia* [note by the writer: soon to be absorbed in the Continentals] who had fled to their homes from Guilford Court-House, cannot be too lavishly extolled. Native courage was common to them all, but they needed discipline, drill, and experience to make them soldiers. It gives me the greatest pleasure to trace the history and march of these patriotic men direct from Guilford Court-House to this bloody baptism of fire at Augusta, and this pleasure will be heightened by the continued observance of their subsequent glorious achievement at Eutaw Springs."

It is of interest to note here that Captains James Read and Edward Yarborough, and Lieutenant John Campbell, of the Continentals, were in the command of Major Eaton, and continued in the service upon the reorganization effected under General Sumner.

The First Regiment, under Colonel John B. Ashe, absorbed ninety of Major Eaton's command, being all that Major Armstrong could find of them, for they seem to have been scattered in several detachments. He also absorbed the command of Major Armstrong, who had been wounded in a duel with Major Lewis and was temporarily disabled.

From the 6th of April to the 1st of August, 1781, North Carolina had sent forward one thousand men to serve as Continentals. Many of them, however, were forced Tories who deserted on receipt of the bounty, the number being reduced, through this cause and by disease, to about eight hundred men, whom we find, in August, 1781, under Colonel John B. Ashe, Major John Armstrong, and Major Reading Blount, as part of General Sumner's brigade of regulars and militia, in General Greene's camp, at the High Hills of the Santee, receiving military training for the battle of Eutaw Springs.

General Greene now felt strong enough to meet the enemy in battle. He broke camp at the High Hills of the

READING BLOUNT.

1756-'8-1807.

Santee, August 23, 1781, and marched towards the enemy at Eutaw Springs, then under the command of Colonel Stewart. The approach of General Greene was unknown to the British, who were posted in an admirable position, which it was not thought the Americans would attempt to attack. Greene's advance guard surprised and captured a foraging party gathering sweet potatoes. His order of battle was the same as at Guilford,—the militia in the first and the Continentals in the second line, on the right of which was Sumner's brigade. In no battle of the war did the militia perform more brilliant service. They seemed anxious to make amends for all former failures and show that all they had needed were drill and discipline. Many of them were those who had abandoned the field at Guilford, but at Eutaw they behaved with such gallantry that nearly two-thirds in action were killed or wounded. When, however, they were forced to retreat, Sumner's brigade was brought forward to their support. Sumner's men came up gallantly and, overpowered by numbers, the British line sullenly retreated. As they fell back in sight of the North Carolina Continentals, General Sumner gave the commond, " Forward, my men, and give them the bayonet!" and the battalions of Ashe, Armstrong, and Blount were pushed forward so promptly that the line was restored and the British left compelled to retreat. It was then that General Greene gave the order to the Maryland Continentals: " Let Williams advance and sweep the field with his bayonets." General Greene reported of Sumner's brigade in this action as follows: " The North Carolina brigade under Sumner, though not above three months raised, behaved nobly. I am at a loss which most to admire, the gallantry of the officers or the good conduct of the men." And again he says of all his troops: "I cannot forbear praising the conduct and courage of all my troops. Never did men or officers offer their blood more willingly in the service of their country."

By the gallantry of Major Majoribanks, a brave and skilful British officer, the tide of American victory was checked. Each side could claim the victory, but the fruits of it fell to the Americans, for the British, after destroying their stores and a thousand muskets, abandoned many wounded and retreated to their sea-coast defences. The British power in South Carolina was completely prostrated by this battle, for, independent of losses incurred, the enemy lost the charm of imputed invincibility in the field. The Americans had learned dependence upon the bayonet, to the full use of which General Greene attributed this victory.

The battle of Eutaw, the crowning exploit of the North Carolina Continentals, is a fitting period to approach the conclusion of this imperfect sketch, for on that field more than half the dead and wounded were North Carolinians.

By the 15th of October, 1781, Greene's camp was re-established at the High Hills of the Santee, Generals Pickens, Marion, and Hampton resuming their partisan operations. On the 9th of November, 1781, the news of Cornwallis's surrender at Yorktown reached General Greene's camp. That camp was abandoned November 18, and numerous minor operations concluded the Southern Campaign of 1781. By an order of General Sumner, dated Camp, Southern Army, Pompon, South Carolina, February 6, 1782, a Board of officers, of the North Carolina line, was convened "to regiment the officers of said line." It provided for four regiments, and included, in the re-organization, some officers who were prisoners of war in captivity or on parole and not yet exchanged. Official reports show that, on April 7, 1782, General Sumner's brigade then contained one thousand one hundred and fifty-four men, and that the terms of service of one thousand of them would expire by January 1, 1783. Upon the reduction of the army, January 1, 1783, only one regiment was retained, and many of the officers were retired from service; some were furloughed "on waiting orders;" but it was not until the latter part of 1783 that all of the North Carolinians were retired and relieved from further service.

To Major Graham Daves, of New Bern, North Carolina, I am under great obligation for most valuable assistance in the compilation of this brief history.

REGISTER OF NORTH CAROLINA OFFICERS

OF THE

CONTINENTAL ARMY

1775 to 1783.

COMPILED BY BREVET MAJOR CHAS. L. DAVIS, U. S. A.

[NOTE.—Those in *italics* continued to the close of the war or were deranged by Acts of Congress. Those in SMALL CAPITALS were members of the North Carolina Society of the Cincinnati.]

MAJOR-GENERAL.

HOWE, ROBERT, Colonel, Second, September 1, 1775; Brigadier-General, Continental Army, March 1, 1776; Major-General, October 20, 1777; died November 12, 1785.

BRIGADIER-GENERALS.

Hogun, James (also spelled Hogan), Major, Georgia Militia, May, 1776; Colonel, Seventh North Carolina, November 26, 1776; Brigadier-General, Continental Army, January 9, 1779; prisoner at Charleston, May 12, 1780; died January 4, 1781, in captivity.

Moore, James, Colonel, First, September 1, 1775; Brigadier-General, Continental Army, March 1, 1776; died January 15, 1777.

Nash, Francis, Lieutenant-Colonel, First, September 1, 1775; Colonel, April 10, 1776; Brigadier-General, Continental Army, February 5, 1777; died October 7, 1777, of wounds received October 4, 1777, at Germantown.

SUMNER, JETHRO, Colonel, Third, April 15, 1776; Brigadier-General, Continental Army, January 9, 1779; died March, 1785.

COLONELS.

Armstrong, James, Captain, Second, September 1, 1775; Colonel, Eighth, November 26, 1776, to June 1, 1778; Colonel, North Carolina Rangers; wounded at Stone Ferry, June 20, 1779.

Buncombe, Edward, Colonel, Fifth, April 15, 1776; died in captivity at Philadelphia of wounds received October 4, 1777, at Germantown.

CLARK, THOMAS, Major, First, September 1, 1775; Lieutenant-Colonel, April 10, 1776; Colonel, February 5, 1777; prisoner at Charleston, May 12, 1780; retired January 1, 1783; Brevet Brigadier-General, September, 1783; died December 25, 1792.

Craick, Thomas, Deputy Commissary-General, November 23, 1776.

HAWKINS, BENJAMIN, of General Washington's staff; died June 6, 1816.

Hawkins, Joseph, died 1785.

Lamb, Gideon, Major, Sixth, April 15, 1776; Lieutenant-Colonel, May, 1776; Colonel, January 26, 1777.

Lillington, Alexander, Colonel, Sixth, April 15, 1776; resigned May, 1776; Brigadier-General of Militia, 1776 to 1782; died 1786.

Long, Nicholas, Deputy Quartermaster-General, May, 1776.

Martin, Alexander, Lieutenant-Colonel, Second, September 1, 1775; Colonel, April 10, 1776; resigned November 22, 1777; died November 12, 1807.

Patton, John, Major, Second, September 1, 1775; Lieutenant-Colonel, April 10, 1776; Colonel, November 22, 1777; prisoner at Charleston, May 12, 1780; retired January 1, 1783.

Polk, Thomas, Colonel of Minute-Men, December 21, 1775; Colonel, Fourth, April 15, 1776; resigned June 26, 1778; died 1793.

Rochester, Nathaniel, Deputy Commissary-General, May 10, 1776; resigned November 23, 1776.

Shephard, Abraham, Colonel, Tenth, April 17, 1777.

Williams, John P., Captain, Fifth, April 17, 1776; Colonel, Ninth, November 26, 1776.

LIEUTENANT-COLONELS.

Alston, William, Lieutenant-Colonel, Third, April 15, 1776, to October 4, 1777.

Armstrong, John, Captain, Second, September 1, 1775; Major, Fourth, October 6, 1777; Deputy Adjutant-General to General Gates, August 3, 1780; Lieutenant-Colonel, Fourth, July 17, 1782; retired January 1, 1783.

ASHE, JOHN BAPTISTA, Captain, First, April 16, 1776; Major, Sixth, January 26, 1777; transferred to First, June 1, 1778; Lieutenant-Colonel, November 2, 1778; died November 27, 1802.

Brewster, Lott, Lieutenant-Colonel, Third, October 25, 1777; resigned March 15, 1778.

Davidson, William Lee, Major, Fourth, April 15, 1776; Lieutenant-Colonel, Fifth, October 4, 1777; transferred to First, June 9, 1779; Brigadier-General of Militia; killed at Cowan's Ford, February 1, 1781.

Davis, William, Captain, First, September 1, 1775; Major, April 10, 1776; Lieutenant-Colonel, February 5, 1777; transferred to ———, June 1, 1778.

Dawson, Levi, Major, Fifth, April 15, 1776; Lieutenant-Colonel, First, February 5, 1777.

Dixon, Henry, Captain, First, September 1, 1775; Major, Third, July 8, 1777; Lieutenant-Colonel, Third, May 12, 1778; wounded at Stone Ferry, June 20, 1779; Colonel, Militia, August, 1780; in Second in 1782; died July 17, 1782.

Harney, Selby, Major, Eighth, November 26, 1776; Lieutenant-Colonel, Second, November 22, 1777; prisoner at Charleston, May 12, 1780; in Third in 1782; retired January 1, 1783.

Ingram, James, Lieutenant-Colonel, Eighth, November 27, 1776; resigned, 1777.

Irwin, Henry, Lieutenant-Colonel, Fifth, April 15, 1776; killed at Germantown, October 4, 1777.

Lockhart, Samuel, Major, Third, April 15, 1776; Lieutenant-Colonel, Eighth, October 12, 1777; resigned October 19, 1777.

Luttrel, John, Lieutenant-Colonel, Ninth, November 27, 1776.

Lytle, Archibald, Captain, Sixth, April 16, 1776; Lieutenant-Colonel, January 26, 1777; wounded at Stone Ferry, June 20, 1779; prisoner at Charleston, May 12, 1780; transferred to First, February 1, 1781; in Fourth in 1782.

Mebane, Robert, Lieutenant-Colonel, Seventh, November 26, 1776; transferred to First, June 1, 1778; Lieutenant-Colonel, commandant Third, June 7, 1779; prisoner at Charleston, May 12, 1780.

MURFREE, HARDY, Captain, Second, September 1, 1775; Major, February 1, 1777; Lieutenant-Colonel, April 1, 1778; in First in 1782; died July 6, 1809.

Taylor, William, Lieutenant-Colonel, Sixth, April 15, 1776.

Thackston, James, Lieutenant-Colonel, Fourth, April 15, 1776.

Walker, John, Captain, First, September 1, 1775; Major, April 26, 1777; Lieutenant-Colonel, Aide to General Washington, February 17, 1777; resigned December 22, 1777; died December 2, 1809.

MAJORS.

BLOUNT, READING, Captain, Third, April 16, 1777; Major, Fifth, May 12, 1778; in Second in 1782; died October 13, 1807.

DOHERTY, GEORGE, Lieutenant, Sixth, April 16, 1776; Captain, September 10, 1776; Major, July 17, 1782.

Donoho, Thomas, Lieutenant, Sixth, April 16, 1776; Captain, September 10, 1776; Major, October 13, 1781; in Fourth in 1782.

Eaton, Pinketham, Captain, Third, April 16, 1776; Major, November 22, 1777; killed at Augusta, June 5, 1781.

Emmett, James, Captain, Third, April 16, 1776; Major, First, December 22, 1777; transferred to ——.

Fenner, William, Lieutenant, Second, September 1, 1775; Captain, May 1, 1776; Major, Seventh, October 24, 1777.

Granger, Caleb, Captain, First, September 1, 1775; Major, February 5, 1777; resigned April 26, 1777.

HOGG, THOMAS, Lieutenant, First, September 1, 1775; Captain, April 10, 1776; Major, Fifth, September 19, 1777; transferred to Third, June 1, 1778; prisoner at Charleston, May 12, 1780; exchanged March, 1781; in Third in 1782; Brevet Lieutenant-Colonel.

McREE, GRIFFITH JOHN, Captain, Sixth, April 16, 1776; transferred to First, June 1, 1778; prisoner at Charleston, May 12, 1780; Major, September 11, 1781; in Third in 1782; Brevet Lieutenant-Colonel, September 30, 1783; Captain, Artillerists and Engineers, June 2, 1794; resigned April 24, 1798; died October 3, 1801.

Nelson, John, Captain, Fourth, April 16, 1776; Major, February 3, 1778; prisoner at Charleston, May 12, 1780; exchanged March, 1781; in First in 1782; retired January 1, 1783.

POLK, WILLIAM, Major, Ninth, November 27, 1776; wounded at Germantown, October 4, 1777; Colonel, Militia, 1777 to 1781; died January 4, 1834.

White, John, Captain, Second, September 1, 1775; Major, April 10, 1776; Colonel, Fourth Georgia, February 1, 1777; wounded and a prisoner at Savannah, October 9, 1779; died of wounds soon afterwards.

Williams, William B., Major, First, June 13, 1776.

CAPTAINS.

Alderson, Simeon, Captain, Fifth, April 16, 1776.

Allen, Charles, Ensign, Second, October 20, 1775; Lieutenant, June 8, 1776; Captain, ——, 1777; transferred to Fifth, June 1, 1778.

Allen, Thomas, Captain, First, September 1, 1775; resigned August 15, 1776.

ARMSTRONG, THOMAS, Lieutenant, Fifth, April 16, 1776; Captain, October 25, 1777; transferred to Second, June 1, 1778; wounded and prisoner at Fort Fayette, June 1, 1779; exchanged December, 1779; prisoner at Charleston, May 12, 1780; exchanged July, 1781; in Second in 1782; Brevet Major.

Armstrong, William, Ensign, First, January 4, 1776; Second Lieutenant, April 10, 1776; Lieutenant, January 1, 1777; Captain, August 29, 1777; wounded at Ramsour's Mills, June 20, 1780; in Third in 1782; retired January 1, 1783.

Ashe, John, Jr., Captain, Fourth, April 16, 1776.

ASHE, SAMUEL, JR., Captain, Sixth, April 17, 1776; transferred to Dragoons, March 7, 1777; to January 1, 1781; died ——, 1814.

BACOT, PETER, Ensign, First, September 19, 1776; Second Lieutenant, February 8, 1777; Lieutenant, October 4, 1777; Captain, ——, 1780; prisoner at Charleston, May 12, 1780; exchanged, June, 1781; died August 13, 1821.

Bailey, Benjamin, Lieutenant, Fifth, October 1, 1776; transferred to First, June 1, 1778; Captain, September 8, 1781; in Third in 1782; retired January 1, 1783.

Baker, John, Captain, Seventh, July 6, 1777; transferred to Third, June 1, 1778; Colonel, Militia; wounded at Bulltown Swamp, November 19, 1778.

BALLARD, KEDAR, Lieutenant, Third, April 16, 1777; Captain, October 4, 1777; prisoner at Charleston, May 12, 1780; on parole, August, 1781; in Third in 1782; retired January 1, 1783; Brevet Major; died January 15, 1834.

Barrot, William, Captain, Third, April 16, 1776.

Bell, Green, Captain, Seventh, November 28, 1776.

Blount, James, Captain, Second, September 1, 1775.

Boadley, George, Captain, Third, September 19, 1778.

Bowman, Joshua, Lieutenant, First, September 1, 1775; Captain, September 18, 1776; killed at Ramsour's Mills, June 20, 1780.

BRADLEY, GEE, Lieutenant, Third, May —, 1776; Captain, September 19, 1778; prisoner at Charleston, May 12, 1780; in Third in 1782.

BREVARD, ALEXANDER, Lieutenant, Fourth, December 9, 1776; transferred to First, June 1, 1778; Captain, October 20, 1780; in Third in 1782; retired January 1, 1783.

Brevard, Joel, Captain, Ninth, November 28, 1776.

Brickell, Thomas, Captain, Seventh, November 28, 1776.

Bright, Simon, Captain, Second, September 1, 1775; resigned April, 1776.

Brinkley, William, Captain, Third, April 16, 1776.

Brown, John, Ensign, First, November 15, 1775; Second Lieutenant, January 4, 1776; Lieutenant, July 7, 1776; Captain, April 26, 1777; transferred June 1, 1778, to Dragoons.

Budd, Samuel, Lieutenant, Second, November 11, 1777;

Captain, ———, 1779; prisoner at Charleston, May 12, 1780; exchanged June, 1781; in Second in 1782 as Lieutenant; retired January 1, 1783.

CALLENDER, THOMAS, Ensign, First, June 6, 1776; Lieutenant, July 8, 1777; Captain, May 12, 1780; prisoner at Charleston, May 12, 1780; exchanged June, 1781; in First in 1782; retired January 1, 1783; died August 20, 1828.

Campbell, James, Second Lieutenant, Second, April 19, 1777; Lieutenant, December 21, 1777; Captain, December 14, 1778; mortally wounded at Stone Ferry, June 20, 1779.

Carter, Benjamin, Lieutenant, Fourth, November 22, 1776; Captain, January 1, 1779; in Second in 1782; died January 20, 1830.

Caswell, William, Ensign, Second, September 1, 1775; Captain, Fifth, April 16, 1776.

Chapman, Samuel, Lieutenant, Eighth, November 28, 1776; Captain, April 5, 1779; in Fourth in 1782.

Child, Francis, Lieutenant, Sixth, April 16, 1776; Captain, January 26, 1777; transferred to Third, June 1, 1778; prisoner at Charleston, May 12, 1780.

Clark, Thomas, Captain, Artillery, January 1, 1777.

Cleaveland, Benjamin, Ensign, Second, September 1, 1775; Lieutenant, January, 1776; Captain, November, 1776; Colonel, Militia, August, 1778; died October, 1806.

COLEMAN, BENJAMIN, Captain, Fifth, April 30, 1777; transferred to Second, June 1, 1778; prisoner at Charleston, May 12, 1780; in Second in 1782; Brevet Major.

Coles, William T., Captain, Fourth, April 16, 1776.

Cook, Richard D., Captain, Ninth, November 28, 1776.

Cooke, James, Ensign, Second, September 1, 1775; Captain, Third, April 16, 1776.

Cotten, Josiah, Captain, Seventh, November 28, 1776.

Council, Arthur, Captain, Sixth, April 16, 1776; died 1777.

Council, Robert, Ensign, First, January 4, 1776; Second Lieutenant, July 7, 1776; resigned September 10, 1776; Ensign, First, March 28, 1777; Second Lieutenant, July 8, 1777; Captain, Dragoons, July 1, 1778.

Craddock, John, Ensign, Second, May 3, 1776; Lieutenant, January, 1777; Captain, December 21, 1777; prisoner at Charleston, May 12, 1780; in Second in 1782; on parole until retired, January 1, 1783.

Crawford, Charles, Captain, Second, September 1, 1775.

Darnall, Henry, Captain, Fifth, October 1, 1776.

DAVES, JOHN, Quartermaster, Second, June 7, 1776; Ensign, September 30, 1776; Lieutenant, October 4, 1777; wounded at Stony Point, July 16, 1779; prisoner at Charleston, May 12, 1780; transferred to Third, January 1, 1781; exchanged June, 1781; Captain, September 8, 1781; retired January 1, 1783; died October 12, 1804; Brevet Major.

Davidson, George, Captain, First, September 1, 1775; resigned February 5, 1777.

Dawson, Henry, Captain, Seventh, December 19, 1776; resigned October 11, 1777.

Dayley, Joshua, Lieutenant, Seventh, December 19, 1776; Captain, October 12, 1777.

Dennis, William, Lieutenant, Eighth, November 28, 1776; Captain, September 20, 1777.

DENNY, SAMUEL, Captain.

Dixon, Tilghman, Lieutenant, First, October 20, 1775; Captain, February 15, 1777; prisoner at Charleston, May 12, 1780; exchanged June 14, 1781; in First in 1782; retired January 1, 1783.

Dobson, Captain; killed June 20, 1780, at Ramsour's Mills.

Ely, Eli, Lieutenant, Seventh, December 11, 1776; Captain, October 12, 1777.

Ely, Samuel, Captain, Seventh, December 17, 1776.

Enloe, John, Captain, Fifth, April 16, 1776.

Evans, Thomas, Ensign, Second, June 6, 1776; Lieutenant, July 19, 1776; Adjutant, November 22, 1778; prisoner at Charleston, May 12, 1780; exchanged March, 1781; transferred to First, January 1, 1781; Captain, June 1, 1781; in Fourth in 1782.

Fawn (or Farrow), William, Second Lieutenant, Third, April 15, 1777; Lieutenant, October 4, 1777; Captain, Lieutenant, March 30, 1780; prisoner at Charleston, May 12, 1780; Captain, ———; retired January 1, 1783.

FENNER, ROBERT, Lieutenant, Second, January 1, 1776; Captain, October 4, 1777; prisoner at Charleston, May 12, 1780; in Second in 1782; Brevet Major.

Ferrebee, William, Lieutenant, Seventh, November 28, 1776; Captain, July 1, 1781; in Fourth in 1782.

Gardner, James, Captain, Second, May 1776; resigned May 15, 1777.

Gaston, Robert, Captain, Second, February, 1776.

Gee, James, Lieutenant, Second, September 1, 1775; Captain, May 3, 1776; died November 12, 1777.

Gee, ———, Captain, ———; wounded at Eutaw Springs, September, 8, 1781.

Glover, William, Lieutenant, Sixth, April 16, 1776; Captain, May 7, 1776.

Goodin, Christopher, Captain, Fifth, January, 1779; killed at Eutaw Springs, September 8, 1781.

Goodman, William, Captain, Fourth, October 1, 1776; killed at Eutaw Springs, September 8, 1781.

Granberry, George, Captain, Third, April 16, 1776.

Granberry, Thomas, Captain, Third, April 16, 1776; died May 20, 1830.

Gray, John, Captain, Third, April 16, 1776.

Green, William, Captain, First, September 1, 1775; resigned January 4, 1776.

Gregory, Dempsey, Captain, Tenth, April 19, 1777; resigned May 22, 1778.

Groves, William, Lieutenant, Fifth, April 15, 1776; Captain, August 17, 1777.

Gurley, William, Captain, Eighth, November 28, 1776.

HADLEY, JOSHUA, Ensign, Sixth, April 16, 1776; Lieutenant, April 1, 1777; Captain, June 13, 1779; wounded at Eutaw Springs, September 8, 1781; in First in 1782; died February 8, 1830.

HALL, CLEMENT, Lieutenant, Second, September 1, 1775; Captain, April 19, 1777; in Second in 1782; Brevet Major; died August 4, 1824.

Hall, James, Captain, Ninth, May, 1777.

Hargett, Frederick, Captain, Eighth, November 28, 1776.

Harris, Thomas, Captain, Fourth, April 16, 1776.

Henderson, Michael, Captain, Ninth, November 28, 1776.

Heritage, John, Lieutenant, Second, September 1, 1775; Captain, May 3, 1776; resigned May 15, 1777.

Heron, Armwell, Captain, Tenth, April 19, 1777.

Ingles, John, Lieutenant, Second, May 3, 1776; Captain, October 24, 1777; prisoner at Charleston, May 12, 1780; in Second in 1782.

James, John, Captain, Sixth, April 16, 1776.

Jarvis, John, Captain, Tenth, April 19, 1777.

Jones, Daniel, Captain, Third, May, 1776; omitted June, 1778.

Jones, Samuel, Lieutenant, Sixth, January, 1777; Captain, 1781.

Jones, Samuel, Lieutenant, Tenth, October 4, 1777; transferred to Third, 1779; Captain, September 11, 1781; retired January 1, 1783.

Keais, Nathaniel, Captain, Second, September 1, 1775.

King, James, Ensign, First, June 1, 1776; Second Lieutenant, August 15, 1776; Lieutenant, April 3, 1777; Captain, March 30, 1780; prisoner at Charleston, May 12, 1780; died in captivity.

Kingsbury, John, Captain, Independent Company Artillery, July 19, 1777; prisoner at Charleston, May 12, 1780.

Lewis, Micajah, Captain, Fourth, July 25, 1777; wounded at King's Mountain, October 7, 1780; Major of Militia; killed, 1781.

LITTLE, WILLIAM (spelled also Lytle), Lieutenant, Sixth, April 16, 1776; Captain, January 28, 1779; transferred to First, January, 1781; in Fourth in 1782.

Maclaine, John, Captain, Fourth, April 16, 1776.

Macon, John, Lieutenant, Seventh, November 28, 1776; Captain, December 11, 1776.

Madearis, John, Lieutenant, Third, April 15, 1777; Captain, December 23, 1777; in First in 1782.

Martin, James, Lieutenant, Second, May 3, 1776; Captain, April 20, 1777; transferred to Fifth, June 1, 1778.

May, James, Jr., Captain, Eighth, November 28, 1776.

McCrory, Thomas, Captain, Ninth, November 28, 1776.

McGlaughan, John, Captain, Seventh, November 28, 1776.

McNees, John, Second Lieutenant, Third, February, 1777; Lieutenant, November 20, 1777; prisoner at Charleston, May 12, 1780; exchanged June, 1781; Captain, ———; transferred to First, January 1, 1781; in Third as Lieutenant in 1782.

Medici, Cosmo, Captain Light Horse.

Mills, James, Captain, Tenth, June, 1779.

Mitchell, George, Captain, Sixth, April 16, 1776.

MONTFORD, JOSEPH, Lieutenant, Third, May, 1776; Captain, January 9, 1779; prisoner at Charleston, May 12, 1780; Captain, First United States Infantry, June 3, 1790; killed, April 27, 1792, by Indians, near Fort Jefferson, Ohio.

Moore, Alfred, Captain, First, September 1, 1775; resigned, March 8, 1777; died October 15, 1810.

Moore, Elijah, Lieutenant, Tenth, October 12, 1777; transferred to First, September, 1778; Captain, October 13, 1781; retired January 1, 1783.

Moore, Isaac, Captain, Tenth, April 19, 1777; transferred to First, June 1, 1778; died July 10, 1778.

Moore, Roger, Captain, Fourth, April 16, 1776.

Neale, Henry, Ensign, First, September 1, 1775; Second Lieutenant, January 4, 1776; Lieutenant, March 28, 1776; Captain, February 5, 1777; resigned April 3, 1777.

Nichols, C. or E., Captain, Third.

Nixon, Thomas, Captain, Eighth, November 28, 1776; resigned September 20, 1777.

Payne, Michael, Captain, Second, September 1, 1775.

Pearl, James, Ensign, Eighth, November 28, 1776; Lieutenant, October 29, 1777; Captain, July 17, 1780; in First as Lieutenant in 1782; retired January 1, 1783.

Phifer, Martin, Captain, Light Horse, March, 1777, to April, 1780.

Philips, Joseph, Captain, Fourth, April 16, 1776.

Pickett, William, Captain, First, September 1, 1775, to January 4, 1776.

Pike, Benjamin, Lieutenant, Sixth, April 16, 1776; Captain, April 28, 1777.

Pope, Henry, Ensign, First, September 1, 1775; Captain, Eighth, November 28, 1776.

Porterfield, Dennis, Captain, Fifth, February 1, 1779; killed at Eutaw Springs, September 8, 1781.

Poynter, John, Captain, Seventh, November 28, 1776.

Quinn, Michael, Lieutenant, Third, January, 1777; Captain, Eighth, August 1, 1777.

RAIFORD, ROBERT, Captain, Eighth, November 28, 1776; in Second in 1782; Brevet Major.

Ramsey, Matthew, Captain, Ninth, November 28, 1776; in Fourth in 1782.

READ, JAMES, Ensign, First, January 4, 1776; Second Lieutenant, July 6, 1776; Lieutenant, July 7, 1776; Captain, July 8, 1777; prisoner at Charleston, May 12, 1780; Brevet Major.

Reed, Jesse, Second Lieutenant, Sixth, October 20, 1776; Lieutenant, October 25, 1777; transferred to Second, June 1, 1778; prisoner at Charleston, May 12, 1780; exchanged June 14, 1781; prisoner at Eutaw Springs, September 8, 1781; Captain, October 15, 1781; in Third in 1782; retired January 1, 1783.

RHODES, JOSEPH T., Captain, Tenth, August 1, 1777; wounded at Stone Ferry, June 20, 1779; in Fourth in 1782; Brevet Major.

Rice, Hezekiah, Lieutenant, First, 1775; Captain, November 28, 1776; omitted January, 1778.

Rochel, John, Captain, Ninth, November 28, 1776; omitted January, 1778.

Rolston, Robert, Ensign, First, September 1, 1775; Second Lieutenant, January 4, 1776; Lieutenant, March 28, 1776; Captain, March 8, 1777; resigned August 29, 1777.

Rowan, Robert, Captain, First, September 1, 1775; resigned June 29, 1776.

Saunders, Jesse, Captain, Sixth, April 16, 1776; resigned May, 1776.

Scull, John Gambier, Ensign, First, June 1, 1776; Lieutenant, November 21, 1776; Captain, April 26, 1777; in service in 1780.

SHARP, ANTHONY, Lieutenant, Ninth, November 28, 1776; Captain, August 24, 1777, in Fourth in 1782; Brevet Major.

Shephard, William, Captain, Tenth, January 20, 1778.

Simons, Peter, Captain, Fifth, April 16, 1776.
SLAUGHTER JOHN, Captain.
Smith, Robert, Lieutenant, Second, September 1, 1775; Captain, Fourth, April 16, 1776; Colonel of Militia.
Standin, Thomas, Ensign, Second, October 20, 1775; Lieutenant, May 3, 1776; Captain, ——; resigned May 15, 1777.
Stedman, Benjamin, Captain, Fifth, April 16, 1776.
Stevenson, Silas, Captain, Tenth, April 19, 1777.
Stewart, Charles, Lieutenant, Fifth, July 23, 1777; transferred to Second, June 1, 1778; prisoner at Charleston, May 12, 1780; Captain, May 18, 1781; in Second in 1782.
Summers, John, Ensign, First, March 28, 1776; Second Lieutenant, July 7, 1776; Lieutenant, February 5, 1777; Captain, July 10, 1778; prisoner at Williamson's Plantation, July 12, 1780; in First in 1782; retired January 1, 1783.
Tarrant, Manlove, Ensign, Second, May 3, 1776; Lieutenant, June 8, 1776; Captain, October 24, 1777; transferred to ——, June 1, 1778.
Tartanson, Francis, Captain, Eighth, January 16, 1777.
Tate, Joseph, Lieutenant, Second, September 1, 1775; Captain, ——, 1776; died June 2, 1777.
Tatum, Absolom, Lieutenant, First, September 1, 1775; Captain, June 29, 1776; resigned September 19, 1776.
TATUM, HOWELL, Ensign, First, September 1, 1775; Second Lieutenant, January 4, 1776; Lieutenant, March 28, 1776; Captain, April 3, 1777; prisoner at Charleston, May 12, 1780; exchanged June 14, 1781; in First in 1782; on parole to close of war; Brevet Major.

Taylor, Philip, Captain, Sixth, April 16, 1776.

Thompson, Lawrence, Lieutenant, First, September 1, 1775; Captain, August 15, 1776; transferred to ——.

Tool, Henry Irwin, Captain, Second, September 1, 1775; resigned April, 1776.

Turner, Jacob, Captain, Third, April 16, 1776; killed at Germantown, October 4, 1777.

Vail, Edward, Lieutenant, Second, September 1, 1775; Captain, August 21, 1776; cashiered December 21, 1777.

Vanoy, Andrew, Captain, Tenth, April 19, 1777.

Vaughan, James, Lieutenant, Seventh, November 28, 1776; Captain, December 19, 1776.

Wade, Joseph J., Captain, Ninth, November 28, 1776.

Walker, Joseph, Captain, Seventh, November 28, 1776.

Walsh, John, Captain, Eighth, November 28, 1776.

Walton, William, Second Lieutenant, Seventh, April 20, 1777; transferred to First, June 1, 1778; Lieutenant, August 15, 1778; prisoner at Charleston, May 12, 1780; exchanged April, 1781; Captain, August 1, 1781; in First in 1782; retired January 1, 1783.

Ward, Edward, Captain, Eighth, November 28, 1776; resigned August 1, 1777.

Ward, William, Captain, Fifth, April 16, 1776.

White, Thomas, Lieutenant, Sixth, April 16, 1776; Captain, January 20, 1777.

Williams, Benjamin, Lieutenant, Second, September 1, 1775; Captain, July 19, 1776.

Williams, Daniel, Lieutenant, Sixth, April 16, 1776; Captain, April 1, 1777; transferred to Third, June 1, 1778.

Williams, James, Lieutenant, Fourth, June 7, 1776; Captain, April 3, 1777; Colonel, Rangers; killed at King's Mountain, October 7, 1780.

WILLIAMS, WILLIAM, Lieutenant and Adjutant, First, September 1, 1775; Captain, Invalid Regiment, April 1, 1778; retired June, 1783.

Wilson, James, Captain, Tenth, April 19, 1777; resigned May, 1778.

Wood, Matthew, Lieutenant, Third, July 24, 1776; Captain, November 22, 1777.

YARBOROUGH, EDWARD, Ensign, Third, May 8, 1776; Lieutenant, April 16, 1777; Captain, May 10, 1779; in Third in 1782; retired January 1, 1783.

LIEUTENANTS.

Alexander, Charles, Lieutenant, Fourth, January 20, 1777.

ALEXANDER, WILLIAM, Ensign, Tenth, May 10, 1781; Lieutenant, September 8, 1781; in Fourth in 1782.

Allen, John, Lieutenant, Fifth, October 1, 1776.

Allen, Thomas, Lieutenant, Third, March 17, 1778; prisoner at Charleston, May 12, 1780; died in prison, August 26, 1780.

Allen, Walter, Ensign, Fifth, March 28, 1777; Lieutenant, October 4, 1777.

Amis, Thomas, Commissary, Third, December 22, 1776.

Andrews, Richard, Ensign, Second, November 1, 1777; Second Lieutenant, March, 1778; prisoner at Fort Fayette, June 1, 1779; Lieutenant, May 10, 1780; exchanged March 26, 1781; wounded at Eutaw Springs, September 8, 1781; in Second in 1782.

Armstrong, Andrew, Lieutenant, Sixth, April 16, 1776.

Ashe, Samuel, Jr., Ensign, Sixth, April, 1779; Lieutenant, ——, 1780; prisoner at Charleston, May 12, 1780; exchanged June 14, 1781; in Ninth (Tenth?) in January, 1781, and Third in 1782; died 1835.

Baker, Peter, Lieutenant, First, February 8, 1777.

Barber, William, Lieutenant, Tenth, April 19, 1777.

Barrow, Jacob, Lieutenant, Seventh, December 22, 1776.

Barrow, Samuel, Lieutenant, Seventh, November 28, 1776.

Beeks, William, Adjutant, Seventh, November 22, 1777.

BELL, ROBERT, Lieutenant, First, September 8, 1781; in Second in 1782.

Berryhill, William, Lieutenant, First, September 1, 1775.

Blount, Jesse, Commissary, Eighth, December 11, 1776.

Blount, Thomas, Lieutenant, Fifth, April 28, 1777.

Blythe, Samuel, Ensign, First, March 28, 1776; Second Lieutenant, July 7, 1776; Lieutenant, February 5, 1777; resigned May 16, 1778.

Brandon, William, Lieutenant, First, September 1, 1775; resigned March, 1776.

Brevard, John, Lieutenant, Ninth, November 28, 1776.

BREVARD, JOSEPH, Lieutenant, First, before March, 1780; Lieutenant, Tenth, August 1, 1781; in Third in 1782.

Brown, Morgan, Lieutenant, Ninth, November 28, 1776.

Bryan, Hardy, Commissary, Seventh, December 11, 1776.

Bryant, John, Jr., Lieutenant, Seventh, November 28, 1776.

Buford, William, Ensign, First Troop, Dragoons, July 16, 1777, to January 1, 1779.

54 REGISTER OF NORTH CAROLINA OFFICERS

Bullock, Daniel, Lieutenant, Ninth, November 28, 1776.

Bush, John, Adjutant, Eighth, August 7, 1781.

BUSH, WILLIAM, Adjutant, Eighth, May 12, 1781.

CAMPBELL, JOHN, Lieutenant, Tenth, April 5, 1779; in Fourth in 1782.

Campbell, John, Second Lieutenant, Second, Continental Artillery, June 29, 1781 to June, 1783.

CAMPEN, JAMES, Ensign, Second, December 11, 1776; Lieutenant, December 21, 1777; wounded and a prisoner at Charleston, May 12, 1780; exchanged June 14, 1781; in Second in 1782; Brevet Captain.

Cannon, Lewis, Lieutenant, Tenth, April 19, 1777.

Carnes, Thomas J., Lieutenant, Artillery, January 1, 1777; resigned March 8, 1779.

Carraway, Gideon, Lieutenant, Eighth, November 28, 1776.

CLARK, THOMAS, Ensign, Ninth, November 28, 1776; Lieutenant, February 10, 1779; in Fourth in 1782.

Clendennin, John, Lieutenant, Third, December 23, 1777; Quartermaster, December 14, 1779; prisoner at Charleston, May 12, 1780; exchanged, June 14, 1781; in Third in 1782.

Coffield, Benjamin, Adjutant, Sixth, May 17, 1777.

Coleman, Theophilus, Lieutenant, Seventh, November 28, 1776.

Colgrave, Arthur, Lieutenant, Second, March 26, 1776. (See Cotgrave.)

Colman, Charles, Quartermaster, Third, October 14, 1777.

Conger, Stephen, Adjutant, First, January 29, 1778; retired June 1, 1778.

Cook, George, Second Lieutenant, Tenth, April 19, 1777; Lieutenant, July 10, 1777; transferred to First, June 1, 1778; prisoner at Charleston, May 12, 1780.

Cooper, Solomon, Lieutenant, Tenth, January 20, 1778.

Cooper, William, Lieutenant, Fifth, April 16, 1776.

Coots, James, Lieutenant, Fourth, November 20, 1776.

Cotgrave, Arthur (also called Anthony); Lieutenant, Second, March 26, 1777; prisoner at Charleston, May 12, 1780; exchanged June 14, 1781; in Second in 1782.

Covington, James, Lieutenant, Ninth, November 28, 1776.

Covington, William, Adjutant, Fourth, March 28, 1777.

Cowan, David, Lieutenant, Tenth, March 20, 1779.

Crafton, Benjamin, Adjutant, Sixth, April 15, 1776.

Craven, James, Ensign, First, June 12, 1776; Second Lieutenant, January 1, 1777; Lieutenant, July 28, 1777; discharged November 20, 1779.

Crutches, Anthony, Ensign, Fifth, February 27, 1780; Lieutenant, May 18, 1781; in Second in 1782.

Curtis, John, Lieutenant, Fifth, October 1, 1776.

Daniel, James, Lieutenant, Ninth, November 28, 1776.

Davis, Abraham, Adjutant, Seventh, December 22, 1776; resigned November 21, 1777; name also spelled Dawes.

Dawes, Josiah, Quartermaster, Seventh, July 10, 1777.

DeKeyser, Lehansyus, Adjutant, First, November, 15, 1775; Second Lieutenant, January 4, 1776; Lieutenant, February 3, 1776; resigned December 10, 1776.

Dent, William, Commissary, Ninth, December 11, 1776.

Dickenson, Richard, Ensign, Sixth, April 2, 1777; Lieutenant, October 10, 1777; transferred to First, June 1, 1778; dismissed November 20, 1779.

Dickerson, Nathaniel, Lieutenant, Ninth, November 28, 1776.

Diggs, Anthony, Lieutenant, Fifth, August 20, 1777.

Dillain, John, Lieutenant, Tenth, February, 1779.

Dillon, Benjamin, Lieutenant, Seventh, October 12, 1777.

Dillon, James, Second Lieutenant, Seventh, January, 1777; Lieutenant, October 12, 1777; transferred to Second, June 1, 1778; killed at Eutaw Springs, September 8, 1781.

Dixon, Charles, Ensign, Sixth, April 2, 1777; Paymaster, January 19, 1778; transferred to Third, July 1, 1778; Lieutenant, February 8, 1779; wounded at Eutaw Springs, September 8, 1781; in Fourth in 1782; retired January 1, 1783.

DIXON, WYNN, Lieutenant, Tenth, July 5, 1781; in Fourth in 1782; died November 24, 1829.

Dobbins, Hugh, Lieutenant, Ninth, ——, 1777.

Douglass, William, Quartermaster, Fourth, February 10, 1777.

Dudley, Thomas, Musician, Sixth in 1776; Ensign, Tenth, 1778; Lieutenant, June 20, 1779; wounded at Eutaw Springs, September 8, 1781; in Third in 1782; retired January 1, 1783.

Eason, Seth, Lieutenant, Seventh, November 28, 1776.

Eborne, John, Lieutenant, Fifth, October 1, 1776.

Eborne, Thomas, Lieutenant, Fifth, April 16, 1776.

Ewell, William, Lieutenant, Fifth, April 20, 1777.

Faircloth, William, Lieutenant, Tenth, January 20, 1778.

FENNER, RICHARD, Paymaster, Second, June 1, 1778; Ensign, January 10, 1779; prisoner at Charleston, May 12,

1780; exchanged June 14, 1781; Lieutenant, May 12, 1781; in Second in 1782.

Ferrebee, Joseph, Lieutenant, Tenth, May 5, 1777.

Ferrell, Luke L., Lieutenant, Tenth, ——, 1778.

Ferrill, William, Lieutenant, Second, September 8, 1777; also in Tenth.

FINNEY, THOMAS, Ensign, Second, November 12, 1777; prisoner at Charleston, May 12, 1780; Lieutenant, January 23, 1781; exchanged June 14, 1781; in Second in 1782.

Foakes, Yelverton, Quartermaster, First, February 3, 1776; resigned August 1, 1776.

FORD, JOHN (also spelled Foard), Ensign, Third, November 30, 1778; prisoner at Charleston, May 12, 1780; exchanged June 14, 1781; Lieutenant, Tenth, January 23, 1781; in Third in 1782.

Foreman, Caleb, Lieutenant, Eighth, November 28, 1776.

Gambelle, Edmund, Ensign, First, March 28, 1776; Second Lieutenant, July 7, 1776; Lieutenant, January 20, 1777; transferred to Dragoons, June 1, 1778.

Gardner, William, Ensign, Second, September 1, 1775; Lieutenant, October 20, 1775.

Gatling, Levi, Lieutenant, Tenth, February 12, 1778; transferred to Second, June 1, 1778; cashiered August 18, 1778.

Gee, Howell, Ensign, Seventh, April 15, 1777; Lieutenant, November, 1777.

Gerald, Charles, Ensign, Fifth, April 30, 1777; Lieutenant, September 19, 1777.

GERRARD, CHARLES, Lieutenant, Second, June 1, 1778; transferred to Fifth ——; transferred to First, January

1, 1781; wounded and prisoner at Charleston, May 12, 1780; exchanged June 14, 1781; in Second in 1782; spelled also Garrard.

Gillespie, Robert, Ensign, Fourth, 1777; Lieutenant, August, 1777.

Godfrey, William, Lieutenant, Eighth, November 28, 1776; resigned August 15, 1777.

Graham, Richard, Lieutenant, Second, June 8, 1776.

Grainger, John, Lieutenant, Second, September 1, 1775.

Granberry, John, Lieutenant, Third, ——, 1777.

GRAVES, FRANCIS, Quartermaster, Eighth, September 1, 1777; Ensign, Third, October 26, 1777; Quartermaster, Tenth, November 6, 1778; Lieutenant, July 14, 1779; prisoner at Charleston, May 12, 1780; exchanged June 14, 1781; in Third in 1782.

Green, Joseph, Commissary, Eighth, December 11, 1776.

Greer, Robert, Lieutenant, Eighth, November 28, 1776.

Hair, John, Lieutenant, First, August 16, 1777.

Hall, Thomas, Ensign, First, December 24, 1776; Lieutenant, February 8, 1777; resigned April 3, 1777.

Handcock, William, Lieutenant, Sixth, April 28, 1777.

Hargrave, William, Ensign, Tenth, January 16, 1778; transferred to First, June 1, 1778; Lieutenant, March 30, 1780; prisoner at Charleston, May 12, 1780; exchanged June 14, 1781; in First in 1782; retired January 1, 1783.

Harris, West, Lieutenant, Ninth, November 28, 1776.

Harrison, William, Ensign, Seventh, December 11, 1776; Second Lieutenant, January, 1777; Lieutenant, July 15, 1777.

Hart, Anthony, Ensign, Third, April 15, 1777; Lieutenant, November 22, 1777; Adjutant, 1778; prisoner at Charleston, May 12, 1780; exchanged, June 14, 1781; in Third in 1782.

Hart, John, Lieutenant, Sixth, May 7, 1776.

Hart, Samuel, Lieutenant, Ninth, November 28, 1776.

Hart, Thomas, Commissary, Sixth, April 23, 1776.

Hays, James, Lieutenant, Seventh, November 28, 1776.

HAYS, ROBERT, Ensign, Fourth, August 16, 1777; Second Lieutenant, October 9, 1777; transferred to First, June 1, 1778; Lieutenant, February 16, 1780; prisoner at Charleston, May 12, 1780; exchanged June 14, 1781; in First in 1782.

Henderson, Pleasant, Lieutenant, Sixth, April 16, 1776.

Hewell, William, Lieutenant, Fifth, March 28, 1777.

Hickman, William, Lieutenant, Fourth, ———, 1777.

HILL, JOHN, Ensign, Tenth, April 4, 1781; Lieutenant, July 5, 1781; in Fourth in 1782.

Hill, William, Lieutenant, First, September 1, 1775.

Hilton, William, Lieutenant, Sixth, April 1, 1777; killed at Stony Point, July 15, 1779.

Hodges, John, Ensign, Fifth, May 4, 1776; Lieutenant, October 1, 1776.

Hodgton, Alvery, Lieutenant, Third, ———, 1777; Adjutant, ———, 1777.

Holland, Spier, Ensign, Fifth, March 24, 1776; Lieutenant, October 25, 1777.

Hollingsworth, Charles, Lieutenant, Fourth, ———.

Hollowell, Samuel, Lieutenant, Eighth, September 20, 1777.

HOLMES, HARDY, Lieutenant, Tenth, ———, 1781.

IVEY, CURTIS, Ensign, Fifth, April 23, 1777; Second Lieutenant, October 10, 1777; Lieutenant, February 1, 1779; in Fourth in 1782.

Ivory, Curtis, Ensign, Third, December 19, 1777; Lieutenant, 1778; was in service in 1780.

Jacobs, John, Ensign, Second, June 6, 1776; Lieutenant, November 1, 1776; resigned March 1, 1778.

Johnson, James, Quartermaster, Sixth, April 2, 1777.

Johnson, Joseph, Lieutenant, First, February 1, 1779; prisoner at Charleston, May 12, 1780; in First in 1782.

Johnson, Joshua, Lieutenant, Ninth, November 28, 1776.

Jones, David, Lieutenant, Fourth, April 3, 1777.

Jones, Maurice, Lieutenant, Sixth, June 15, 1776.

Jones, Philip, Lieutenant, Artillery, July 19, 1777; prisoner at Charleston, May 12, 1780.

Jones, Philip, Lieutenant, Eighth, November 28, 1776.

Jones, Timothy, Lieutenant, Tenth, April 19, 1777.

Jones, Thomas, Lieutenant, Seventh, April 17, 1777.

Kennon, John, Lieutenant, Sixth, April 16, 1776.

Kennon, William, Commissary, First, September 23, 1776; resigned April, 1777.

Knott, William, Lieutenant, Fourth, ——, 1777.

Koen, Caleb, Lieutenant, Tenth, April 19, 1777.

Lackey, Christopher, Lieutenant, Third, ——, 1777.

LAMB, ABNER, Ensign, First, ——, 1780; Lieutenant, June 1, 1781; wounded at Eutaw Springs, September 8, 1781; in First in 1782.

Langford, Alloway, Ensign, Eighth, February 8, 1777; Lieutenant, August 1, 1777.

Lassiter, Jethro, Ensign, Seventh, November 28, 1776;

Second Lieutenant, January, 1777; Lieutenant, October 12, 1777.

Lawrence, Nathaniel, Ensign, Second, June 1, 1777; Lieutenant, Tenth, June 1, 1778; prisoner at Charleston, May 12, 1780; exchanged April 18, 1781; in Second in 1782 as Lieutenant, January 23, 1781, with name spelled Nathan Lawrence.

Lewis, Joel, Lieutenant, Tenth, August 1, 1779; wounded at King's Mountain, October 7, 1780.

Lewis, Joseph, Lieutenant, Eighth, November 28, 1776.

Lewis, William, Lieutenant, Ninth, March, 1777.

Lillington, John, Lieutenant, First, September 1, 1775; resigned May, 1776; Colonel of Militia, 1779 to 1782.

Linton, William, Lieutenant, Third, July 24, 1776.

Lockey, Christopher, Lieutenant, Fifth, May 3, 1776.

Long, Nehemiah, Lieutenant, Fifth, October 4, 1776.

Love, Amos, Lieutenant, Sixth, April 16, 1776.

Lowe, John, Lieutenant, Tenth, April 19, 1777.

Lowe, Philip, Ensign, Second, September 1, 1775; Lieutenant, May 3, 1776; resigned February 1, 1777; Major, Third Georgia, June 18, 1778; Lieutenant-Colonel, ——; retired January 1, 1781.

Luton, James, Ensign, Second, April 1, 1777; Lieutenant, October 4, 1777; resigned March 10, 1778.

Lynch, John, Lieutenant, Seventh, November 28, 1776.

Lytle, Micajah, Lieutenant, Third, May 3, 1776.

Mallett, Daniel, Commissary, Fourth, December 16, 1776.

Mallett, Peter, Commissary, Fifth, April 23, 1776.

Marshall, Dixon, Ensign, First, March 28, 1777; Second Lieutenant, April 26, 1777; Lieutenant, July —, 1779;

62 REGISTER OF NORTH CAROLINA OFFICERS

prisoner at Charleston, May 12, 1780; exchanged June 14, 1781; died August 22, 1824.

Martin, Samuel, Lieutenant, Second, June 8, 1776.

Mason, Richard, Ensign, Second, September 4, 1778; Lieutenant, 1780.

McAlister, Neil, Ensign, First, September 1, 1775; Second Lieutenant, January 4, 1776; Lieutenant, June 29, 1776; resigned January 20, 1777.

McCanley, Matthew, Lieutenant, Tenth, April 19, 1777.

McCann, John, Lieutenant, Sixth, April 16, 1776.

McGibbony, Patrick, Ensign, Fourth, November 27, 1776; Lieutenant, December 9, 1776.

McIlwaine, Stringer, Lieutenant, Second, ———, 1777. (See McKlewaine.)

McNaughton, John, Lieutenant, Eighth, November 28, 1776.

McNeill, Hector, Lieutenant, First, September 1, 1775; deserted February 3, 1776.

McSheehy, Miles, Adjutant, Ninth, February 12, 1777.

Messick, Jacob, Ensign, Eighth, November 18, 1776; Lieutenant, April 24, 1777.

Milligan, James, Ensign, First, March 28, 1777; Second Lieutenant, April 23, 1777; Lieutenant, August 29, 1777; dismissed July 13, 1778, by sentence of a court-martial.

Mills, Benjamin, Lieutenant, Eighth, January, 1777; resigned July 12, 1777; Lieutenant, Dragoons, July 15, 1777.

Moore, Dempsey, Lieutenant, Sixth, April 16, 1776.

MOORE, JAMES, Ensign, First, ———, 1780; Lieutenant, July 1, 1781; wounded at Eutaw Springs, September 8, 1781; in First in 1782.

Moore, John, Lieutenant, Seventh, December 17, 1776.

Moorehead, James, Lieutenant, Tenth, March 23, 1779.

Moslander, Abel, Lieutenant, Fourth, January 25, 1777.

Myrick, John, Ensign, Seventh, November 28, 1776; Lieutenant, December 11, 1776.

Nash, Clement, Lieutenant, Second, May 3, 1776; resigned February 1, 1777; Captain, Third Georgia, April 10, 1777; prisoner at Briar Creek, March 3, 1779; exchanged ———, prisoner at Charleston, May 12, 1780.

Neal, William, Lieutenant, Ninth, November 28, 1776.

Nicholson, Robert, Lieutenant, Tenth, April 19, 1777; transferred to First, June 1, 1778; resigned June 25, 1779; died May 21, 1819.

Noblen, William, Lieutenant, Seventh, November 28, 1776.

Nuthall, Nathaniel, Ensign, Ninth, May 20, 1777; Adjutant, May 26, 1777.

O'Neal, Charles, Ensign, Third, April 18, 1777; Lieutenant, July 20, 1777.

Owen, Stephen, Lieutenant, Eighth, August 15, 1777.

Owens, John, Lieutenant, Sixth, May 7, 1776.

Parker, Kedar, Ensign, Sixth, May 7, 1776; Lieutenant, September 19, 1776.

Parkinson, James, Lieutenant, Second, 1777; died March 26, 1778; spelled also Parkerson.

Pasteur, John, Lieutenant, Sixth, July 7, 1776.

PASTEUR, THOMAS, Ensign, Fourth, July 15, 1777; Lieutenant, December 29, 1777; transferred to First, June 1, 1778; Adjutant, June 26, 1779; prisoner at Charleston, May 12, 1780; exchanged June 14, 1781; in First by the arrangement of February 6, 1782; Paymaster, Fourth, October 19, 1782; Lieutenant of Infantry, United States Army, June 3, 1790; Captain, First United States Infantry, March 5, 1792; in First Sub-Legion, September 4, 1792; in First United States Infantry, November 1, 1796; Major, Second Infantry, April 11, 1803; died July 29, 1806.

Polk, Charles, Lieutenant, Fourth, April 25, 1777.

Polk, Thomas, Lieutenant, ———; killed at Eutaw, September 8, 1781.

Pollock, Jacob, Lieutenant, Fourth, ———, 1776.

Powers, James, Lieutenant, Seventh, November 28, 1776.

Powers, James, Lieutenant, Third, April 20, 1777.

Pyeatt, Peter, Lieutenant, Tenth, March 30, 1781.

Raiford, John, Lieutenant, Second, ———, 1777; resigned February 1, 1778; spelled also Radford.

Ramsay, Allen, Lieutenant, Seventh, December 19, 1776.

Redpeth, John, Lieutenant, Fourth, August 20, 1777; killed October 13, 1777.

Reese, George, Lieutenant, Ninth, November 28, 1776.

Respess, Richard, Lieutenant, Eighth, November 28, 1776.

Rice, John, Adjutant, First, December 10, 1776; Ensign, March 28, 1777; Second Lieutenant, April 3, 1777; First Lieutenant, First Continental Dragoons, June 1, 1778.

Roberts, John, Lieutenant, Fifth, March 28, 1777; transferred to Second, June 1, 1778.

Rochel, Lovick, Lieutenant, Third, November 28, 1776; resigned November, 1777.

Rogers, Patrick, Quartermaster, First, November 3, 1776; Ensign, March 28, 1777; Lieutenant, April 3, 1777; died April 19, 1778.

Rolston, Isaac, Ensign, Second, June 8, 1776; Lieutenant, ——, 1777; transferred to ——, June 1, 1778.

Ross, Francis, Lieutenant, Ninth, November 28, 1776.

Roulledge, William, Lieutenant, Fourth, January 25, 1777; resigned August 20, 1777.

Rountree, Reuben, Lieutenant, Tenth, April 19, 1777.

Rushworm, William, Lieutenant, Third, April 16, 1777.

Salter, James, Commissary, Second, December 19, 1776.

Salter, Robert, Commissary, Second, April 23, 1776.

SAUNDERS, WILLIAM, Ensign, Sixth, April 2, 1777; transferred to First, June 1, 1778; Lieutenant, February 8, 1779; in Fourth in 1782; retired January 1, 1783.

Sawyer, Levi, Second Lieutenant, Second, May 15, 1776; Lieutenant, ——, 1777; resigned March 16, 1778.

Scurlock, James, Lieutenant, Tenth, September 11, 1781; in Fourth in 1782.

Shaw, Daniel, Ensign, Sixth, April 2, 1777; Second Lieutenant, October 11, 1777; transferred to First, June 1, 1778; Quartermaster, June 2, 1778; prisoner at Charleston, May 12, 1780; exchanged June 14, 1781.

Singleton, Richard, Lieutenant, Second, June 17, 1775.

Singleton, William, Lieutenant, Eighth, November 28, 1776; resigned October 26, 1777.

Slade, Stephen, Quartermaster, Second, January 1, 1778; prisoner at Charleston, May 12, 1780; Lieutenant, January 23, 1781; exchanged June 14, 1781; in Second in 1782.

Slade, William, Ensign, Fourth, January 2, 1777; Lieutenant, May 1, 1777; transferred to First, June 1, 1778; Adjutant, June 1, 1778; resigned February 18, 1780.

Smith, Jabez, Lieutenant, Fifth, September 1, 1777.

Snowden, Nathaniel, Lieutenant, Tenth, June 5, 1778.

Snowden, William, Lieutenant, Seventh, November 28, 1776.

Southall, Stephen, Second Lieutenant, Second, April 1, 1777; also in Tenth; Lieutenant, First Continental Artillery, ——, 1780; retired January 1, 1783.

Southerland, Ransome, Commissary, Fourth, April 23, 1776.

Spratt, Thomas, Lieutenant, Ninth, November 28, 1776.

STEED, JESSE, Lieutenant, Tenth, September 8, 1781; in First in 1782.

Stewart, George, Lieutenant, Ninth, November 28, 1776.

Stewart, Joseph, Lieutenant, Ninth, November 28, 1776.

Stewart, Nicholas, Lieutenant, Second, April 30, 1777.

Sugg, George, Lieutenant, Fifth, ——, 1776.

Swann, Nimrod, Quartermaster, Fifth, June 8, 1777.

Tatum, James, Ensign, Ninth, August 12, 1777; Second Lieutenant, January 1, 1778; Lieutenant, December 14, 1779; prisoner at Charleston, May 12, 1780; exchanged June 14, 1781; in Third in 1782; on parole to close of war; died September 10, 1821.

Thompson, Samuel, Lieutenant, Sixth, April 16, 1776.

Tillery, John, Lieutenant, Third, ——, 1777.

Turbee, William, Lieutenant, Third, July 6, 1777.

Turner, Robert, Lieutenant, Tenth, ——, 1778.

Vance, David, Lieutenant, Second, April 20, 1776; transferred to ——, June 1, 1778.

Vance, John C., Second Lieutenant, Artillery, July 19, 1777; Lieutenant, July 8, 1779; prisoner at Charleston, May 12, 1780; exchanged June 14, 1781.

Van Duyck, John, Lieutenant, Artillery, February 1, 1777.

Varcase, James, Lieutenant, Tenth, March 17, 1778.

Varner, Robert, Ensign, First, March 28, 1776; Second Lieutenant, July 7, 1776; Lieutenant, March 8, 1777; cashiered October 1, 1779.

Verner, James, Lieutenant, First, May 8, 1777.

Verrier, James, Ensign, Fifth, August 20, 1777; Lieutenant, June, 1778.

Walker, Solomon, Lieutenant, Sixth, April 20, 1777.

Walker, William, Lieutenant, Second, ——; prisoner at Charleston, May 12, 1780; exchanged June 14, 1781.

Wall, James, Lieutenant, Artillery, July 19, 1777.

Wallace, James, Lieutenant, Tenth, November 30, 1778.

Walters, William, Ensign, First, September 19, 1776; Second Lieutenant, February 5, 1777; Lieutenant, September 19, 1777; transferred to cavalry, June 1, 1778.

Washington, Robert, Adjutant, Third, April 15, 1776.

Watson, Thomas, Lieutenant, Seventh, November 28, 1776.

Webb, John, Commissary, Third, April 23, 1776.

Whedbee, Richard, Lieutenant, Seventh, November 28, 1776.

White, Matthew, Lieutenant, Sixth, ——, 1777.

Whitmel, Blunt, Lieutenant, Fourth, November 20, 1776.

Wilkinson, Reuben, Ensign, Fourth, December 9, 1776; Lieutenant, January 9, 1779; in Third in 1782.

Williams, John, Lieutenant, Second, April 21, 1777; transferred to ——, June 1, 1778.

Williams, Nathaniel, Lieutenant, Tenth, January, 1782; in Fourth in 1782, with commission dating January 23, 1781.

Williams, Nathaniel B., Lieutenant, Eighth, November 28, 1776; retired January 1, 1783.

Williams, Ralph, Lieutenant, Ninth, November 28, 1776.

Wilson, Whitfield, Quartermaster, Third, April 24, 1777.

Womack, William, Quartermaster, First, January, 1778; dropped by rearrangement June 1, 1778.

Wood, Solomon, Lieutenant, Eighth, November 28, 1776.

Worth, Joseph, Ensign, Second, October 20, 1775; Lieutenant, May 3, 1776; died April 6, 1777.

Wright, David, Ensign, Tenth, April 19, 1777; Lieutenant, February 15, 1778; transferred to First, June 1, 1778.

Yancey, Charles, Lieutenant, Ninth, November 28, 1776.

ENSIGNS OR SECOND LIEUTENANTS.

Alderson, Thomas, Ensign, Fifth, May 3, 1776.

Bertie, Thomas, Ensign, Eighth, November 28, 1776.

Bickerstaff, John, Ensign, Second, June 8, 1776.

Blanton, Rowland, Ensign, Eighth, November 28, 1776.

Brice, Peter, Ensign, Ninth, November 28, 1776.

Bryer, Benjamin, Ensign, Seventh, April 27, 1777; Second Lieutenant, July 15, 1777.

Carpenter, Peter, Ensign, Eighth, November 28, 1776.

Caustariphen, James, Ensign, Seventh, November 28, 1776.

Cawall, Butler, Ensign, Tenth, ——.

Charlton, William, Ensign, Tenth, March 14, 1779; mortally wounded at Stono Ferry, June 10, 1779.

Cheese, John, Ensign, First, June 12, 1776; Second Lieutenant, January 20, 1777; resigned April 1, 1777.

Cheeseboro, John, Paymaster, July 3, 1777; Ensign, Sixth, April 25, 1779.

Childs, James, Ensign, First, September 1, 1775.

Clinch, James (also spelled Joseph), Ensign, Second, September 1, 1775.

Coleman, John, Ensign, Ninth, November 28, 1776.

Crawford, David, Ensign, First, June 10, 1777.

Crawford, William, Ensign, First, January 4, 1776; Second Lieutenant, March 28, 1776; resigned August 15, 1776.

Crenshaw, Arthur, Ensign, Second, ——; prisoner at Charleston, May 12, 1780; exchanged June 14, 1781.

Crutches, Henry, Ensign, Fifth, August 20, 1777.

Curtis, Joshua, Ensign, Fourth, July 1, 1777; resigned February 1, 1778.

Curtis, Reuben, Ensign, Second, ——, 1777.

Curtis, Thomas, Ensign, Eighth, November 28, 1776.

Dance, Ethelred, Ensign, ——, 1781; died February 4, 1828.

Daniel, Stephen, Ensign, First, January 4, 1776; resigned June 3, 1776.

Douglass, Robert, Third Lieutenant, Artillery, July 19, 1776.

Eagle, Joseph, Ensign, Fourth, January 4, 1776; resigned March 20, 1776.

Erwin, John, Ensign, First, ——, 1777.

Ferrall, Micajah, Ensign, Ninth, November 28, 1776.

Gibson, Thomas, Ensign, Tenth, February 20, 1780; prisoner at Charleston, May 12, 1780; exchanged June 14, 1781.

Graham, George, Ensign, First, September 1, 1775; Second Lieutenant, January 4, 1776; resigned April 15, 1776; Captain, North Carolina Rangers.

Grant, Reuben, Ensign, Sixth, April 16, 1776.
Grant, Thomas, Ensign, Sixth, April 16, 1776.
Hicks, William, Ensign, Ninth, November 28, 1776.
Irwin, John, Ensign, First, March 28, 1777; Second Lieutenant, April 4, 1777; resigned August 28, 1777; Colonel, Militia, in 1780 and 1781.
Johnston, Joseph, Ensign, Ninth, November 28, 1776.
Jones, Samuel, Ensign, Second, ——; died July, 1778.
Killeby, William Tyler, Ensign, Second, ——; died April 6, 1777.
Lacey, John, Ensign, Second, May 20, 1779.
Lanier (or Lenear), James, Jr., Ensign, Eighth, November 28, 1776; resigned October 12, 1777.
Lemmy, Joseph, Ensign, First, January 4, 1776; Second Lieutenant, January 18, 1776; died July, 1776. (See McLemmy.)
Liscombe, John, Ensign, Sixth, April 28, 1777.
Loomis, Abner, Ensign, Eighth, February 8, 1776; resigned November 15, 1777.
McCarthy, Florence, Ensign, Fourth, May 1, 1777.
McClammy, Joseph, Ensign, Second, October 20, 1775.
McDougall, James, Cornet of Dragoons.
McKinne, James, Ensign, Fifth, May 9, 1776.
McKlewaine, Samuel, Second Lieutenant, Second, May, 1776; resigned October 24, 1777. (See McIlwaine.)
McLemmy, Joseph, Ensign, First, January 4, 1776; Second Lieutenant, January 18, 1776; died July, 1776. (See Lemmy.)
McRenolds, Robert, Ensign, Tenth, April 19, 1777.
McRory, James, Ensign, Ninth, May 2, 1777.

Mercer, John, Ensign, Seventh, November 28, 1776; resigned November 22, 1777.

Moore, Maurice, Jr., Ensign, First, September 1, 1775; Second Lieutenant, January 4, 1776; killed January 18, 1776.

Morgan, Benjamin, Ensign, Third, ——, 1776.

Mossom, Richard, Ensign, Tenth, September 4, 1778.

Murray, William, Ensign, Fourth, April 1, 1777.

Nelson, Alexander, Ensign, Fourth, July 1, 1777.

Oliver, John, Ensign, Second, September 1, 1775.

Orrell, Thomas, Ensign, Tenth, March 14, 1778.

Outlaw, Edward, Ensign, Sixth, April 16, 1776.

Palmer, Joseph, Ensign, Fifth, June 6, 1776.

Pearce, George, Ensign, Ninth, November 28, 1776.

Picket, Thomas, Ensign, First, October 20, 1775.

Pilley, John, Ensign, Second, December 11, 1776.

Pugh, Whitmel, Ensign, Second, September 1, 1775.

Respess, John, Ensign, Eighth, November 28, 1776.

Rice, Jeptha, Ensign, Ninth, March 15, 1777.

Richardson, John, Ensign, Tenth, October 1, 1777.

Robinson, Septimus, Ensign, First, March 28, 1776; Second Lieutenant, July 7, 1776; resigned August 10, 1776.

Sawyer, William, Ensign, Second, May 15, 1776.

Shute, Thomas, Ensign, Tenth, April 19, 1777; omitted by arrangement of June 1, 1778; died January 15, 1819.

Singleton, Robert, Ensign, Tenth, ——.

Sledge, Arthur, Ensign, Seventh, December 19, 1776.

Smith, John, Ensign, Ninth, November 28, 1776.

Sutton, James, Second Lieutenant, Second, ——; resigned March 10, 1778.

Taylor, John, Ensign, First, September 1, 1775.
Thomas, John, Ensign, Ninth, November 28, 1776.
Tochsey, William, Ensign, Second, May 3, 1776.
Triplet, Charles, Ensign, First, September 19, 1776; died December, 1776.
Turner, Berryman, Ensign, First, September 1, 1775.
Vipon, Henry, Ensign, Second, September 1, 1775.
Washington, William, Ensign, Ninth, August 15, 1777.
Watters, Samuel, Ensign, First, December 24, 1776; Second Lieutenant, March 29, 1777; resigned April 23, 1777.
Webb, Elisha, Ensign, Seventh, November 28, 1776.
Whitaker, Hudson, Ensign, Seventh, December 22, 1776.
White, William, Ensign, Seventh, April 17, 1777.
Williams, Theophilus, Ensign, Sixth, April 2, 1777.
Woodhouse, John, Ensign, Second, September 1, 1775.
Wooton, Shadrack, Ensign, Fifth, ——, 1776.

PAYMASTERS.

Alexander, Hezekiah, Paymaster, Fourth, April 16, 1776.
Ashe, Samuel, Paymaster, First, September 1, 1775; resigned April 16, 1776; President of State Council of Safety, 1776; died 1843.
BLOUNT, JACOB, Paymaster, State Troops, April 18, 1776.
Blount, William, Paymaster, Third, ——, 1777.
Bradley, Richard, Paymaster, Third, March 5, 1777; retired June 1, 1778.
Duncan, Robert, Paymaster, Fourth, December 1, 1777.
Guion, Isaac, Surgeon, First, September 1, 1775; resigned December, 1775; Paymaster, March, 1777, to July, 1778.
Harvey, James, Paymaster, Seventh, December 11, 1776.

Lord, William, Paymaster, First, December 11, 1776; resigned March 5, 1777.

Moseley, William, Paymaster, Sixth, December 11, 1776.

Pasteur, William, Surgeon, Second, September 1, 1775; Paymaster, Fourth, December 12, 1776.

Rogers, John, Jr., Paymaster, Fifth, December 11, 1776.

Spicer, John, Paymaster, Second, December 11, 1776.

Taylor, John, Paymaster, Eighth, July 24, 1777.

SURGEONS AND SURGEONS' MATES.

Alexander, Nathaniel, Surgeon, 1778 to 1782; died March 8, 1808.

Blythe, Joseph, Surgeon, First, July, 1776; prisoner at Charleston, May 12, 1780; exchanged June 14, 1781; in Fourth in 1782.

Boyd, Hugh, Surgeon, Fourth, April 17, 1776.

Brevard, Ephraim, Surgeon, First, ——; prisoner at Charleston, May 12, 1780.

Cooley, Samuel, Surgeon, Fifth, April 16, 1776.

FERGUS, JAMES, Surgeon, First, May 24, 1776; resigned April, 1777; also called John; spelled as Forgus, he appears as Surgeon's Mate, Tenth, February 21, 1782; Surgeon, August 20, 1782.

Geikee, James, Surgeon, First, December, 1775; resigned May, 1776.

Green, James W., Surgeon's Mate, Tenth, June 10, 1778; Surgeon, December 7, 1779; prisoner at Charleston, May 12, 1780; exchanged June 14, 1781; in First in 1782.

Hall, Robert, Surgeon, Third, April 17, 1776.

Halling, Solomon, Surgeon, ——.

Hamilton, Hanse, Surgeon, Seventh, April, 1777.

Helmburg, Frederick, Surgeon, First, March 13, 1778.

Johnston, Lancelot, Surgeon, Ninth, December 22, 1776.

Loomis, Jonathan, Surgeon, Eighth, November 26, 1776; prisoner at Charleston, May 12, 1780; exchanged June 14, 1781; in Third in 1782.

Love, David, Surgeon, North Carolina brigade, August 18, 1779, to August 1, 1781.

McClure, William, Surgeon, Sixth, April 17, 1776; prisoner at Charleston, May 12, 1780; exchanged June, 1781; in Second in 1782.

Parton, William, Surgeon, Second, September 1, 1775.

Ridley, William, Surgeon, Third, April 21, 1777.

Usher, William, Surgeon, Third, December 4, 1776; and of Fourth, April 24, 1777.

Wilson, Robert, Surgeon, Sixth, June 8, 1776.

Blackley, Ebenezer, Surgeon's Mate, Tenth, ——, 1778.

Bull, Thomas, Surgeon's Mate, Tenth, 1782.

McLane (also McClaine and Maclaine), WILLIAM, Surgeon's Mate, Tenth, January 1, 1783; died October 25, 1828.

Moore, William, Surgeon's Mate, Tenth, January 19, 1778.

CHAPLAINS.

Atkin, James, Chaplain, Fourth, April 5, 1777.

BOYD, ADAM, Ensign, First, January 4, 1776; Second Lieutenant, March 3, 1776; resigned May, 1776; Chaplain, Second, October 1, 1777; Brigade Chaplain, August 18, 1778, to June 1, 1778; died 1800.

Foard, Hezekiah, Chaplain, Fifth, April 20, 1777.

Tate, James, Chaplain, First, October 13, 1775; Brigade Chaplain, June 1, 1778.

DIPLOMA OF JOHN DAVES, CAPTAIN NORTH CAROLINA CONTINENTAL LINE, AND MEMBER OF THE NORTH CAROLINA STATE SOCIETY OF THE CINCINNATI.—FROM THE ORIGINAL IN THE POSSESSION OF HIS DESCENDANT, MAJOR GRAHAM DAVES, NEWBERN, N. C.

A SKETCH
OF THE
NORTH CAROLINA SOCIETY
OF THE
CINCINNATI.

PREFACE.

In the following sketch the author does not pretend to originality. The nature of the subject renders it impossible. The history of the causes which led to the formation, as well as the institution itself, of the Society of the Cincinnati has been frequently written by abler pens than his, while the brief record of the North Carolina State Society has been already narrated by one who was a sincere lover of both the Order and the "old North State,"—Professor Edward Graham Daves. For years it had been his earnest wish and constant endeavor, as the grandson and representative of Major John Daves, one of the original members of the North Carolina Society and himself an honored member of the Maryland Cincinnati, that the Society in his native State should be revived. But death terminated his labors ere their completion. His brother, Major Graham Daves, of New Bern, has nobly taken up the task as far as possible where it was relinquished, and it is sincerely hoped may yet, with others, be enabled to carry on the patriotic work to its full conclusion.

With an earnest wish of assistance, the undersigned has therefore only endeavored, at the risk of repetition, to aid in such good work by narrating, for convenience, in combined form the brief history and record of this association of patriots as already written by those who have preceded him. To these latter-named, rather than to the present writer, is the credit due for the preservation and rescue from oblivion of the following data.

H. H. BELLAS.

October 31, 1895.

A SKETCH

OF THE

NORTH CAROLINA SOCIETY OF THE CINCINNATI.

BY HENRY HOBART BELLAS, LL.B.,
CAPTAIN U. S. ARMY.

ONE hundred and twelve years ago was one of the most critical, by reason of its being one of the most uncertain periods in our country's early career. It is true, the war of the Revolution had ended; but with so much doubt and distrust prevailing everywhere—both in the rank and file of the American army as well as in all branches of civil life—coupled with the exhausted condition of the nation and its finances; the situation ahead was one to daunt even a patriot Washington.

With that sense of possible coming danger, both to themselves and their beloved country for which they had fought and suffered eight long years, the officers of the American army, both "to perpetuate the friendships they had formed in the past under the pressure of a common danger," as well as to aid each other in the future "by substantial acts of beneficence," and "to promote and cherish that union and honor between the States" so vitally necessary for the preservation of the new government, united themselves, before their final disbandment, into a "Society of Friends" styled THE CINCINNATI, "to endure as long as they shall endure, or any of their male posterity, and in failure thereof, the collateral branches who may be judged worthy of becoming its supporters." *

It was the final embodiment of an idea originally conceived, it is authoritatively stated, as early as the winter of 1778,—nearly five years before the termination of the war, —and announced then for the first time before Washington and his brother-officers in a discourse by the Reverend William Smith, D.D., Provost of the College and Academy of Philadelphia, from the pulpit of old Christ Church, in that city,† afterwards endorsed by Baron von Steuben and other

---

* See original "Institution" of the Cincinnati.

† "On the feast of St. John the Evangelist's Day, December 28, 1778, the celebrated Dr. William Smith, at a service held in this church, at which the Commander-in-Chief of our armies was present, referred to him as the Cincinnatus of America, *voicing then and there for the first time in public*, it is believed, the idea that nearly five years later took shape in the organization of the Society of the Cincinnati." See discourse by Rt. Rev. Wm. Stevens Perry, D.D., LL.D., D.C.L., in Christ Church, Philadelphia, February 21, 1892.

It has, however, it is but fair to state, been held by a recent authority that this reference was but an historical parallel between Washington and his Roman predecessor in the relinquishment of domestic duties at the call of their

1732–1785.

leading officers of the American army, and the plan of final organization drawn by General Knox and others at the close of the war.

One of those to sign the original "Institution" as drafted by the officers named was Major-General Robert Howe,* of Brunswick County, of the State of North Carolina, and whose name appears among the first of the signatures to the instrument. The Society, first formed in cantonment at Newburg, on the banks of the Hudson River, in May, 1783, and perfected during the following month, was gradually extended during the same year through the different States to the southward, in accordance with the recommendation made at the formation of the Society, and by the close of the year Societies were in existence in all of the thirteen States.

---

country, rather than enunciating the idea of the formation of a yet inchoate Society by those who at the *close of the war* followed the example of Cincinnatus by *retirement* to their private citizenship after the deliverance of their country.

* General Robert Howe was born in Brunswick County, North Carolina, in 1732, and died there, November 12, 1785. Returning from England in 1766, he was appointed captain under commission of Governor Tryon, and baron of the exchequer. He was a member of the Assembly in 1772-73, delegate to Colonial Congress of 1774, and chairman of committee to which the speech of the loyal Governor Martin was referred. His services in the Revolution are a matter of well-known history. He was one of the most uncompromising of the patriots of the Cape Fear region, for we find him honored by being excepted from the offer of pardon to "the rebels" by Sir Henry Clinton in 1776. He served to the close of the war, and was afterwards (1785) appointed by Congress to treat with the western Indians. On his return to North Carolina he was received with public honors and elected to the Legislature, but died soon after.

The North Carolina Society was one of the last to take definite shape, being organized at Hillsborough, in that State, in the latter part of the month of October, with Brigadier-General Jethro Sumner,* of Warren County, as its first president, and Reverend Adam Boyd,† of Wilmington, as secretary, with sixty-one members, or (as we find by comparison) ‡ over one-half of the entire number of " officers of the late war who continued to the end thereof or were deranged by Acts of Congress."

There is probably no military or other Order which

---

* General Sumner was a native of Virginia, and as early as 1760 was appointed a paymaster in the provincial forces of that State and commander of Fort Cumberland. In 1776 he resided in North Carolina, was appointed colonel of a regiment of Continental troops, and joined the Northern army, under the command of Washington. He was promoted brigadier-general in 1779, and served under Gates and Greene in the Southern campaign. He died in Warren County, North Carolina, 1785, and was buried near old Shocco Chapel and Bute Court-House. The following inscription is upon his tombstone: "To the memory of GENERAL JETHRO SUMNER, one of the heroes of '76." (See Wheeler's "History of North Carolina," p. 425.)

General Sumner's sword is deposited in the Tennessee Historical Society at Nashville.

† Rev. Adam Boyd was an ardent patriot from the beginning of the Revolution, and was an active member of the Wilmington (North Carolina) Committee of Safety. He established and published the *Cape Fear Mercury* in October, 1767. This was the paper that printed the celebrated Mecklenburg Declaration of Independence of May 20, 1775, and caused the royal Governor of North Carolina (Governor Martin) to issue his proclamation of August 8, 1775, against the "most infamous publication." See *North Carolina University Magazine*, May, 1895. Chaplain Boyd removed to Natchez, Mississippi, about 1787, where he died in 1800.

‡ See Washington Correspondence, "Archives of Department of State, Washington, D. C.," Book 115, pp. 142½, 143.

originated in more historic surroundings or with more patriotic purposes. Created to strengthen and perpetuate the ties formed in service on many a field of battle for their country's cause, as well as to provide a fund for the indigent and needy in after years, not only among themselves, but for their widows and orphans; its very disinterestedness and honesty of intention served, as has so often since been the case in the history of our country, to excite all the political passion, bitter hostility, and calumny of demagogism which at that period swept the land. The very insignia of the Order—a golden eagle, emblematic of their country,—together with their modest motto, *Omnia relinquit servare rempublicam*, as an evidence of their self-denial, were cited by those hostile to the Society as proofs of the danger to the new government from these self-created aristocrats, as they were styled by their enemies. The principle of primogeniture was probably the most obnoxious of all the features of the Society to the people at large.

The disbandment of the armies, both in the North and South, and the consequent scattering of the officers belonging to the same, necessitated the division of the Society into "State Meetings" for each State, which were to be held annually, while the general body, comprising its general officers and delegates from each State, met triennially for consultation.*

---

* General John Cochrane, President of the New York State Society of the Cincinnati, has in a recent publication shown very clearly the difference between the original powers of the State Societies and the (so-styled) General Society, as well as proving conclusively that the former really constitute the Society of the Cincinnati, in accordance with the intention of the original "In-

Each officer contributed one month's pay* to the formation of a permanent fund in each State Society, the interest alone of which was available for the purposes already indicated.

Claim to membership in the Society originally belonged only to "all the officers of the American army, as well those who have resigned with honor after three years' service in the capacity of officers, or who have been deranged by the resolutions of Congress, upon the several reforms of the Army, as those who shall have continued to the end of the war," . . . "and as a testimony of affection to the memory and the offspring of such officers as have died in the service, their eldest male branches shall have the same right of becoming members as the children of the actual members of the Society." Honorary members, eminent for their abilities and patriotism, were also provided for in the different State Societies, in a ratio not exceeding one to every four hereditary members. Officers who had served in the Continental navy, as well as such officers of State Troops (not Militia) as had served in time and manner indicated, were afterwards

---

stitution," rather than the triennial General Meeting of the representatives from the State Societies, as has been claimed. See second letter of General John Cochrane to the New York Cincinnati, 1895.

* This month's pay was estimated as follows: *Army:* Major-Generals, $180 and $166, respectively. Brigadier-Generals, $125. Colonels and Lieutenant-Colonels commanding Artillery, $100; Cavalry, $93.67; Infantry, $75. Lieutenant-Colonels, $60. Majors, Artillery and Cavalry, $62.45; Infantry, $50. Captains, Artillery and Cavalry, $50; Infantry, $40. Captain-Lieutenants and Lieutenants, Artillery, $33.30; Infantry, $26.60. Chaplains, $75. Surgeons, $59. Surgeons' Mates, $46. [With some variations.]

Navy: Captains, $60. Lieutenants, $30.

recognized by resolution of the General Society, in its first meeting, as also eligible to membership in the Society.*

Such were the principal characteristics of the Society of the Cincinnati as originally organized. At this day and in this generation it is difficult, if not impossible, for us to realize the hostility it aroused in the minds of the hostile, the evil-disposed, and the ignorant. Forgetful altogether of the character and the services of the men composing the Order,—the very men who had saved the nation and created a new government, and who, of all others, should have been free from suspicion or criticism,—a bitter attack was made upon it in almost every State in the Union; an attack led, as is always the case, by those who for personal motives or for political gain hoped to reap advantage thereby.

"Few occurrences of so little comparative importance have ever given rise to so much excitement as the establishment of the Cincinnati," says Johnson in his life of General Greene.† . . . "The hereditary principle and the badge, the alleged mimicry of royal orders, were the avowed object of the attack; but there can be but little doubt that the *excluding rule*, which shut all the rest of the world out of the Society, except commissioned officers of the United States, was the real object of offence." . . . "The exclusive principle was the great ground of complaint. That the hereditary principle or even the bauble at the button-hole were not the real cause of alarm, has since been satisfactorily

---

* See Proceedings of General Society of the Cincinnati, Philadelphia, 1784.

† "Sketches of the Life and Correspondence of Major-General Nathaniel Greene," by William Johnson, Charleston, S. C., 1822, vol. ii., pp. 409-11.

established, for the one was never relinquished (as suggested), and the other has been silently resumed without giving any alarm or doing the least sensible injury." . . . " The people have since had the good sense to find out that *they* have the same right to form Societies and exclude, if they will, the Cincinnati from them; aye, and to wear badges and assert the honors of hereditary perpetuation, and they now bestow an unfeigned tribute of respect on the hoary heads of the few venerable survivors of the Revolutionary officers. When they shall have passed away, it is easy to foresee what will be the fate of the Society."(?) . . .

The writer himself believed "it was an injudicious and injurious measure calculated to offend the popular side!" *

And Moore, in his " History of North Carolina," states that " in the grave and important issues before the people of the State, there was unfortunately a struggle evolved between the lawyers and those who had filled important military commands in the army. There were, as a general rule, strenuous efforts made against the return of the Tories, and that popular prejudice was used as a lever to oust the influence of some who had largely directed public opinion during the war.† The organization of the Society of the

---

* " Sketches of the Life and Correspondence of Major-General Nathaniel Greene," by William Johnson, S. C., 1822, vol. ii., p. 411.

† Surgeon James Tilton, President of the Delaware State Society of the Cincinnati, had stated in the General Meeting of the Society in 1784, in response to the request of Washington, the President-General, to declare the ideas prevalent in the respective States regarding the " Institution," " that the principal and indeed the only enemies of the Cincinnati in his State (Delaware) were among the class of people denominated Tories." See Proceedings

GRIFFITH JOHN McREE.

1758–1801.

Cincinnati by the late officers was viewed by many with distrust as to its aims.". . . "The Federal distresses were incessant and increasing. To the wise and good men of that day, the future was full of painful uncertainty. The grand opportunities of America, seemed to be fading from the possibility of achievement by reason of divided councils, ignoble jealousies, and the insane selfishness of the individual States. Suspicion and detraction poisoned the public mind with unceasing calumnies. The Order of the Cincinnati was at best only a social brotherhood, but was denounced as a conspiracy against the people's liberties, and the *very authors* of American liberty were held up to scorn, as conspirators against the best interests of the nation.

"The 'Patriotic Society'* was a rival organization which sprung up in that day and became in effect greatly similar to the movement under Governor Tryon, known as the Regulation.

" In North Carolina but little permanent interest was taken in either of these organizations, which were soon to sink from public observation." †

Washington, in order to placate the democratic opposition then prevalent, suggested at the first General Meeting of the Society in 1784 that the original "Institution" "be

---

of General Society in Winthrop Sargent's "Journal of Cincinnati General Meeting, 1784." " Penna. Hist. Soc. Pub.," vol. vi., p. 80.

* For account of the " Patriotic Society" Constitution, see " History Delaware State Society of Cincinnati," by Captain H. H. Bellas, Wilmington, Delaware, 1895 (" Delaware Historical Society's Publications," No. xiii., pp. 34, 35).

† See Moore's " History North Carolina," pp. 357–369.

amended by abolishing the principle of hereditary succession; that all interference with political subjects should be done away, and that the funds should be placed under the immediate cognizance of the several State legislatures, who should also be requested to grant charters for more effectually carrying our humane designs into execution." *
Happily, these proposed amendments to the "Institution" as originally adopted, were never fully carried out by all the States, and the principle of hereditary succession still remains in full force to-day.†

In an official letter to General Knox, the Secretary-General, from the Rev. Adam Boyd, Secretary of the North Carolina Society, and dated Wilmington, North Carolina, December 29, 1783, announcement is made of the formation of the North Carolina State organization. A similar letter by General Jethro Sumner (the President) to Major-General Baron de Steuben, dated Halifax, North Carolina, October 28, 1783, together with one of the same date by the Secretary, is also on file with the former letter in the archives of the General Society.‡

As these are the earliest appearing evidences of the existence of this honored Society in the "old North State," it may be of interest as well as value to give their contents entire. General Sumner's letter, being of the earlier date of the two, is first given, and is as follows:

---

* See Circular Letter of General Society in Proceedings of General Meeting of the Cincinnati, Philadelphia, 1784.

† See Report of Committee on "Institution," Proceedings of General Society of Cincinnati, Philadelphia, 1800.

‡ See Proceedings of General Society of Cincinnati, Philadelphia, 1784.

"HALIFAX, N. CAROLINA, 28th. October, 1783.

"SIR :—At the request of the officers of the Line of this State, I do myself the honour to return you their thanks & my own for your favour, covering a letter from his Excellency the Chevalier De la Luzerne, and other papers. The officers being highly pleased with the Institution, will most chearfully concur in any measures that shall be adopted for promoting its benevolent designs. Not to support such an Institution betrays, in their opinion, a want of public virtue.

"It appears to be the sense of the Societies to the Southward, that the first general meeting should be held at Fredericksburg, in Virginia.* That place,

---

* The suggestion in both this and the following letter of the Secretary of the Society that the first general meeting should be held in Fredericksburg, Virginia, did not evidently meet the approval of the President-General, as appears from a letter from him to General Sumner in the beginning of the following year. This letter, the original of which has been presented by the Honorable David Schenck to the Roanoke Colony Memorial Association of North Carolina, reads as follows:

"MOUNT VERNON, Jany 5th, 1784.

"SIR :—After taking all the various circumstances into mature consideration, I have thought proper to appoint the City of Philadelphia to be the place for the general meeting of the Society of the Cincinnati on the first Monday in May next, agreeably to the original Institution. The object of this letter is to communicate timely information thereof, that proper notice may be given to the Delegates of your State Society, whose punctual attendance will be expected at the time and place before mentioned.

"Having made this communication, I have only to suggest that it may perhaps be preferable to give the necessary notice to your Delegates by letter rather than by a public notification; I would, however wish that whatever mode is adopted, measures may be taken to prevent a possibility of failure in the communication.

"I have the honor to be
"Sir
"Your Ob't Hum. Serv't,
Go. WASHINGTON.

"P. S. Be pleased to acknowledge the receipt of this letter.
"Brigadier General Sumner,
"North Carolina."

it is tho't, is nearly centrical, and most convenient for the President-General. The compliance of the Northern Societies in this, will give us very great pleasure.

"I shall always be extremely glad to hear from & to correspond with you, and have the honour to be, with great respect,

"Your most obedient & very humble servant,

"*Brig-Gen'l and President.*

"HON. MAJOR-GENERAL BARON DE STEUBEN."

The Secretary's letter, the first mentioned, is to the following effect:

"WILMINGTON, CAPE FEAR, 29th. Dec'r., 1783.

"SIR:—

"In October a few officers of this State met at Hillsborough & laid the foundation of a society upon the plan of the Cincinnati. Among other things they resolved that the president should acquaint the Secretary-General with their desire, that the first general meeting should be held at Fredericksburg, in Virginia. That place is tho't to be nearly centrical and more convenient than any other for the President-General. This last was most decisive with them.

"The president having been obliged to go home before any letters could have been written, I was desired to write to you on the subject. This I did upon the spot, & gave my letter to a gentleman coming directly here. Since my return to this place I find that letter was lost, and not knowing that General Sumner has had an opportunity of conveying one to you, I again address you, lest the wishes of the N. Carolina Society should not reach you in proper time, and I should incur their censure, tho' very undeservedly.

"A pamphlet said to be the production of a judge Burke in So. Carolina, has created opponents to the Cincinnati. It has been in this town, but I have not yet got a sight of it. His objections, I am told, are founded upon a surmise that the Cincinnati mean to establish a numerous peerage in direct contradiction to the federal union of the States. This he has tortured out of the 'hereditary succession.' The whole appears to me altogether chimerical: but there are swarms of Butterfly-statesmen & patriots, who flutter and strutt in the sunshine of safety & peace. These things affect to be lynx-eyed, and however groundless their cries may be, yet being generally of a popular tone, they are received 'as proofs from holy writ.'

"Terrible things have been threatened against us, & I do expect our Assembly, in their April sessions, will be moved to suppress the Society. At that time we have a meeting, and if you can furnish anything to strengthen our hands, you will render us a very acceptable service.

"As our President lives near 200 miles from a sea-port town or post-office, letters for him had better be sent here I am about to change my place of residence, but if I do leave this, our vice-president (General Clark) and several officers will be here & take care of such letters.

"I have the honour to be, with much respect,

"Your very humble and most obedient servant,

Adam Boyd Sec'y.

"P. S.—I would most gladly correspond with the secretary of your State Society. If you will please tell him so, you will do me a favour. My address is Rev'd A. B., Wilmington, Cape Fear. This is the South part of No. Carolina, & vessels from Boston often come here. If I remove, my address will not be changed.

"HONOURABLE GENERAL KNOX."

No list of members is given, as transmitted with either of the foregoing letters, and the list furnished by the Secretary to the Maryland Society, over a year later, is, he states, still incomplete.* The complete roll, however, at this time, taken from the records in the possession of the General Society, and arranged according to rank, appears as follows:

---

* See letter to General Otho H. Williams, of May 20, 1785, page 95.

Major-General Robert Howe.
Brigadier-General Jethro Sumner.
Colonel and Brevet Brigadier-General Thomas Clark.
Colonel Archibald Lytle.
Lieutenant-Colonel John Baptista Ashe.
Lieutenant-Colonel Hardee Murfree.
Major and Brevet Lieutenant-Colonel Thomas Hogg.

MAJORS.

Griffith John McRee.	Reading Blount.
George Doherty.	William Polk.

CAPTAIN AND BREVET MAJORS.

Thomas Armstrong.	Kedar Ballard.
Benjamin Coleman.	Robert Fenner.
Clement Hall.	Robert Raiford.
James Read.	Joseph T. Rhodes.
Anthony Sharpe.	Howell Tatum.

CAPTAINS.

Samuel Ashe, Jr.	Peter Bacot.
Gee Bradley.	Alexander Brevard.
Thomas Callender.	John Daves.
Samuel Denny.	Joshua Hadley.
William Lytle.	Joseph Montfort.
John Slaughter.	William Williams.

Edward Yarborough.

LIEUTENANT AND BREVET CAPTAIN.

James Campen.

SOCIETY OF THE CINCINNATI. 93

LIEUTENANTS.

William Alexander. Robert Bell.
Joseph Brevard. William Bush.
John Campbell. Thomas Clarke.
Wynne Dixon. Richard Fenner.
Thomas Finney. John Ford.
Charles Gerard. Francis Graves.
Robert Hayes. John Hill.
Hardy Holmes. Curtis Ivey.
Abner Lamb. James Moore.
Thomas Pasteur. William Saunders.
Jesse Steed.
Cornet James McDougall.
Deputy Paymaster-General Jacob Blount.
Surgeon's Mate James Fergus.
Surgeon's Mate William McLane.
Brigade Chaplain Reverend Adam Boyd.

But while the officers of the North Carolina regiments were, on the authority of General Sumner, "highly pleased with the Institution and most cheerfully concurred in any measures that should be adopted for promoting its benevolent designs," the Society met in this, as in other States, with decided opposition from the Legislature. At a meeting of the Society held in Fayetteville on July 4, 1784, the Secretary was ordered to address a circular letter to the other State societies. This communication shows the attitude of the State Assembly towards the organization, as well as reporting the action of the Society on the amendments which had been proposed to the Institution to disarm hostility, at the first General Meeting in Philadelphia, in May of that year, and already alluded to.

The letter is on file in the archives of both the Maryland and Massachusetts Cincinnati Societies:

"CAPE FEAR, No. CAROLINA, 10th Jan'y, 1785.

"SIR:

"I am ordered by the Cincinnati of this State to acquaint you that, in consequence of a former adjournment, we had a meeting at Fayette Ville on the 4th of July (1784), when the circular letter, with the Institution as altered and amended, was read and highly approved.

"The meeting then proceeded to frame their bye-Laws and to make such regulations as they tho't might promote the friendly and benevolent intentions of the Society.

"We had hopes that the Assembly would take our funds under their direction and aid the general design; but tho' the ablest members of both Houses were on our side, yet the majority was against us.

"Waiting the event of this application, I deferred writing and am truly sorry I cannot give a more agreeable account of it. Yet this disappointment will not affect the zeal of our members, and we flatter ourselves the opposition will soon die.

"It is the earnest wish of this meeting to hold correspondence with the different State meetings. This, it is tho't, might be of general advantage and contribute to that harmony which is the soul of the Society.

"I am with much respect,

"Yr. most obedient servant,

"ADAM BOYD, Sec.

"Secretary to the Cincinnati in Maryland."

These by-laws, together with an incomplete roll of the names of the members of the Society, were inclosed in a second letter a few months later (dated May 20, 1785), addressed to General Otho H. Williams, of the Maryland Cincinnati.

The letter reads as follows:

"NEW BERNE, NO. CAROLINA, 20th. May, 1785.

"SIR:—In obedience to orders, you will herewith receive a copy of the bye-laws of this State meeting; and I was likewise ordered to send a copy of the Institution, with the names of our members, on parchment. But the gentleman appointed for that purpose has not sent me the parchment, neither is the roll of names by any means compleat. At our annual meeting I hope these and some other things will be better regulated.

"I beg, Sir, you will excuse the liberty I have taken in troubling you with the enclosed letters. My reason for taking it was, I knew not the name of an officer near a sea-port in your State or Virginia, whither I beg the sealed one may be sent. It is a transcript of that designed for the Secretary of the Maryland meeting.

"I have the honor to be, with the utmost respect,

"Your obedient and most humble servant,

"ADAM BOYD.

"HON'BLE GENL. WILLIAMS, MARYLAND."

The by-laws enclosed number seventeen articles and are of the usual nature of rules for the government of such an organization. One rule (the fourth) was particularly worthy of imitation, however, providing that *copies* of all letters and essays should be recorded by the Secretary, the originals of which must likewise be filed. All proceedings of the Society were directed to be kept *in duplicate*, one of the books of record being kept by the Secretary and the other lodged with the President, being carefully revised and compared with each other at every meeting, to prevent error.*

But how fruitless even all these precautions were for the preservation of the history of this patriotic organization, we shall see later on.

---

* See post, pages 97, 98.

The Society was represented, it would appear, at the meetings of the General Society but three times—in 1784, 1787, and 1790. The delegates to the first General Meeting were Lieutenant-Colonel Archibald Lytle, Major Reading Blount, and Major Griffith John McRee. They were elected at a meeting of the State society held at Hillsborough in the month previous (April), and their certificate of appointment, which is still preserved, has been stated—erroneously, however—to be "the only known evidence in existence that there was a Society of the Cincinnati in North Carolina."

The certificate is as follows:

"NORTH CAROLINA, HILLSBOROUGH, April 18, 1784.

"Lieutenant-Colonel Com't. Lytle, Major Blount and Major McRee are delegated to represent the State Society of the Cincinnati in the general convention to be held in Philadelphia on the first Monday in May next.

"Attested: JETHRO SUMNER, Pres't.
"C. IVEY, Sec'y *pro tem.*"

Of the three above-named delegates, Majors Blount * and McRee attended the meeting of the General Society, the published proceedings of which show that the first-named officer was one of a committee appointed to amend and revise the "Institution" of the Society.† This proposed

---

* Major Reading Blount was born *circa* 1756–'8, and died October 13, 1807. He was a son of Jacob Blount, member of the provincial assemblies of 1755–'6, and descended from Thomas Blount, of Edgecombe County, N. C., and Elizabeth Reading, his wife. Major Blount had several brothers, William, Thomas, and John Gray, all distinguished in political life after the Revolution in North Carolina and Tennessee. For history of the Blount family, see Wheeler's "Reminiscences and Memoirs," pp. 130–'1.

† See Proceedings of General Society of Cincinnati, Philadelphia, 1784.

North Carolina Hillsborough April 16th 1784

Sir,

You are hereby, Major Blount, and Major Elisha... Our delegates to represent the other officers of the Cincinnati in the General Convention to be held in Philadelphia on the first Monday in May next.

Attest:
C. O. Guy Secy pro.tem.   Jno Sumner Pr.

CERTIFICATE OF APPOINTMENT OF DELEGATES OF THE NORTH CAROLINA STATE SOCIETY OF THE CINCINNATI TO THE GENERAL SOCIETY, AT ITS MEETING IN PHILADELPHIA, PA., MAY, 1784.

amended constitution was, as is well known, never carried into effect, failing of ratification by a majority of the different State societies; North Carolina, however, being one of the States which did so approve it.

The place of meeting of the Society on July 4, 1785, appears to have been again at Fayetteville, at which meeting the rules and regulations for governing the State meeting were again reported, evidently revised and completed.

As these by-laws may be of interest to members of the Cincinnati or their descendants to-day, not only in North Carolina, but elsewhere, we present them entire, at the risk of tediousness.

FAYETTEVILLE, NORTH CAROLINA, July 11th, 1785.

RULES AND REGULATIONS FOR GOVERNING THIS STATE MEETING.

I. The first business of the anniversary meeting shall be the election of a President, Vice-President, Secretary, Treasurer and a representation to the Society for the ensuing year. Three members shall be appointed Judges of the election, and any two of said Judges agreeing, shall declare those having a majority duly elected; and in case of an equality of ballots, the decision shall be by lot.

II. All elections shall be by ballot.

III. The President is, at all meetings, to regulate the decision of everything that may be proposed; to state and put questions, agreeably to the sense and intention of the members. He is also empowered whenever he shall think it necessary, to call an extraordinary meeting, on giving sixty days' previous notice by circular letters to the members in each district, and in any occasional absence of the President and Vice-President, the members present shall appoint to the chair one of their number, who, whilst there, shall possess all the power of a President.

IV. The Secretary shall take the minutes of the proceedings of each meeting and produce them, fairly transcribed in a book, to the next meeting. In this book shall also be entered all such letters and Essays addressed to them or the Society as they may think worth recording, the Originals of which must likewise be filed: and the more effectually to guard against accidents, which may endanger the records, the proceedings shall be copied into two books; for one of which the Secretary shall be answerable, and the other shall be lodged with the President, and in Order to prevent errors, those books of record shall be carefully revised and compared at every meeting.

V. The Treasurer shall receive the subscriptions and donations of members, and others, agreeably to the Institution and under the direction of the meeting, shall manage their fund, and transact all their monied matters. He shall also lay before every annual meeting, a true state of the stock, interest, and other monies belonging to them, and disbursements made by their Orders; and he shall deliver to his successor the books and all papers belonging to his Office, together with all monies remaining in his hands. And for the faithful discharge of his trust, the said Treasurer, before he enters on the Duties of his Office, shall give bond and security to the President and Vice-President, on behalf of the meeting, in the sum of five thousand pounds.

VI. At every annual meeting any number of members shall be competent to the business of the meeting, consistant with the rules of the Society.

VII. The transactions of extraordinary meetings shall be binding, until the next annual meeting, which shall have the power to confirm or abolish their proceedings.

VIII. In conducting the business of the meeting, no question shall be put on a motion, unless it be seconded. When any member speaks, he shall address himself to the Chair; and no member without permission shall speak more than twice on the same subject.

IX. No part of the Interest arising from the principal fund, and other monies in the disposal of the meeting, shall be ordered in payment for charitable or other purposes, without the consent of two-thirds of the members present. Each member shall report to the annual meeting such objects of charity as may come within his notice; and agreeably to circumstances, the meeting shall grant orders for such sums of money as shall be judged necessary, and consistant with the state of finances.

X. It shall be the duty of any member elected to an Office in the meeting or Society, to Officiate agreeably to the appointment.

XI. All questions which are not determined by some express Rule, shall be decided by the Voice of a majority of the members present.

XII. Any member who shall fail to attend the annual meeting, shall pay to the Treasurer the sum of five pounds currency, for the use of the meeting, unless his excuse be admitted by a majority of members present.

XIII. The expence of deligation to the Society, and all other necessary expenditures, shall be an equal contribution of the members of the meeting.

XIV. No member shall absent himself without permission from the Service of the meeting.

XV. No member shall be expelled the Society, but by consent of two-thirds of the members present at the annual meeting.

XVI. Should the meeting be reduced to the disagreeable necessity of expelling a member, the motive shall be entered at large on the minutes; and as soon as possible, notice shall be given to the Society by the President, who shall also by circular letter inform the different meetings thereof, specifying his name and situation, previous to his becoming a member.

XVII. These rules and regulations to be subject to any alterations or amendments at an annual meeting, two-thirds of the members agreeing thereto.

(Copy.) ADAM BOYD, *Secy*.

For the following year (1786), the annual stated meeting of the Society was held at Halifax "agreeable to their adjournment from Fayetteville" the preceding year. This meeting is the only one in the brief history of the Society, of which any account exists, as far as known at present, in the newspapers of the day. A copy of the *Pennsylvania Packet and Daily Advertiser* of August 12, 1786, preserved in the archives of the New Jersey State Society, contains a report of the meeting of the North Carolina Society on July 4th. Neither the names, however, of officers elected nor of any members of the Society are mentioned.

The account reads as follows:

"HALIFAX, N. CAROLINA, July 8th. (1786.)

"The State Meeting of the Cincinnati was held here on the 4th, agreeable to their adjournment from Fayetteville; the festivity of this auspicious day commenced by a suitable discharge of artillery about 11 o'clock. A large number of gentlemen from the town and different parts of the State met the Society at Mr. Barkdale's tavern, where an elegant dinner was prepared by the direction of their stewards. After dinner the following toasts were drunk, accompanied by separate discharges of cannon and animated with the most rational mirth and patriotic enthusiasm:

1. The Memorable 4th July, 1776.
2. The United States of America.
3. The late American Army and Navy.
4. The Fleet and Armies of France who have served in America.
5. His Most Christian Majesty.
6. His Excellency General Washington.
7. May America be grateful to her Patriotic Children!
8. The Memory of the Brave Patriots who have fallen in defence of America.
9. May Virtue support what Courage has gained!
10. The Vindicators of the Rights of Mankind in every quarter of the Globe.
11. May America be an Asylum to the Persecuted of the Earth!
12. May a close Union of the States guard the Temple they have erected to Liberty!
13. May the Remembrance of this Day be a Lesson to Princes!

The afternoon was spent in the utmost conviviality, enlivened with a number of gay and political songs and toasts. In the evening the Society gave a ball, which was honoured with a numerous and splendid attendance of the ladies."

On the decease of the President, General Sumner, in the month of March of the preceding year (1785), Lieutenant-Colonel John Baptista Ashe,* of New Hanover County, had

---

* Lieutenant-Colonel John Baptista Ashe was the son of Samuel Ashe, Chief Justice and Governor of North Carolina, and the nephew of General John Ashe, distinguished in the Revolution. Colonel John Baptista Ashe was born in Rocky Point, North Carolina, 1748, and served continuously through the war, especially distinguishing himself at the battle of Eutaw. He was afterwards a

John Baptist Ashe

1748-1802.

been chosen to fill the vacancy. Major Howell Tatum was elected Secretary to succeed Rev. Adam Boyd a couple of years later (1787), and Major Robert Fenner as Treasurer. This last-named officer was the sole representative of the Society at the second triennial meeting of the General Society at Philadelphia in the latter year, the other two delegates, Colonel William Polk* and Major Reading Blount, failing to attend.†

Again, at the third General Meeting of the Society in 1790, the only representative present from North Carolina was Colonel Benjamin Hawkins,‡ of Warren County. The records of that meeting report him as acting on a committee

---

member of the House of Commons of North Carolina (1786), and also of the State Senate (1789 and 1795), a delegate to the last Continental Congress (1787-88), and member of the First and Second Congress (1789-93). In 1802 he was elected Governor of North Carolina, but died before his inauguration. See Memoir of Ashe family, note, page 5, of "History North Carolina Troops of the Continental Army," by Brevet Major Charles L. Davis, U.S.A.

* Lieutenant-Colonel William Polk, who was Major of the Ninth Regiment of North Carolina Continental Infantry, was the son of Colonel Thomas Polk, of Mecklenburg, North Carolina, and was born in the county of Mecklenburg, 1759. He was present at the celebrated Convention held there in May, 1775. Entering the army the following year, he served gallantly through the war, being wounded at both Germantown and Eutaw. At the close he returned to Charlotte, and in 1787 represented his county in the North Carolina Legislature. He afterwards removed to Raleigh, where he resided until his death, January 4, 1834. In 1812, President Madison offered him a brigadier-general's commission, which he declined. Colonel Polk was not only the last surviving member of the North Carolina Society of the Cincinnati, but was also the last surviving field-officer of the North Carolina line in the Revolution.

† See Proceedings of General Society of Cincinnati, Philadelphia, 1787.

‡ Colonel Benjamin Hawkins was born in Warren County, North Carolina, August 15, 1754, and was a student in Princeton College, New Jersey, when

appointed to prepare an address to General Washington, the President-General of the Society, congratulating him "on being unanimously elected the head of our rising republic," as well as informing him of his re-election as President of the Society for the ensuing three years. A circular-letter was prepared by the same committee and forwarded to the different State Societies " on the situation and prospect of the affairs of the United States." *

After this last date no delegates from North Carolina were ever present at the General Meetings, nor, so far as is now known, were there any meetings of the State Society; certainly there is no record of such, nor even of the existence of the Society. No reference, with one exception, is ever made to it in the report of the successive committees appointed by the General Society to inquire into the "present situation of the different State Societies," and to urge those already dormant or dissolved to "a renewal of their intercourse" with the General Society. The exception alluded to was by the committee appointed to examine

---

the Revolution began. His proficiency in French caused General Washington to appoint him interpreter between the American and French officers on his staff. In 1780 he was commissioned to procure ammunition and arms in the West Indies. He was elected to Congress by the North Carolina Legislature in 1782, and in 1785 was appointed to treat with the Cherokee and Creek Indians. He was re-elected to Congress in 1786, and in 1789 became one of the first two United States Senators from North Carolina. He was appointed in 1797 agent for "superintending all Indians south of the Ohio." He tendered his resignation to each successive President from Washington to Madison, but it was always refused. The city of Hawkinsville, Georgia, where he died June 6, 1816, was named in his honor.

* See Proceedings of General Society of Cincinnati, Philadelphia, 1790.

documents, etc., in the possession of officers of the Society, with a view to the publication of such facts as may be of interest, which, at the General Meeting in 1857, after reporting that, "with few exceptions, even the rolls of the several State Societies have disappeared from the archives of the General Society, and such as remain are not wholly to be depended on as accurate," stated in regard to this particular Society under consideration as follows:

"Very diligent inquiry has been made for the North Carolina records, but without avail and without encouragement to hope for final success." *

The finding of the papers of Major Tatum,† the last-known secretary of the Society, might throw some light on this and kindred matters regarding the length of its existence and its proceedings.

When and under what circumstances did the Society become dormant? for it cannot justly, from the nature of its institution, be said to have ceased to exist.‡

---

* See Proceedings of General Society of Cincinnati, Boston, Massachusetts, 1857.

† Major Howell Tatum subsequently removed to Tennessee; was Treasurer of the Western District of that State, 1794-96; Attorney-General of same, 1796-97; Supreme Court Judge, May 12, 1797, to September 20, 1798, and was afterwards (*circa* 1807) one of the Commissioners to adjust the land claims between Tennessee and North Carolina. His descendants are residents of Tennessee to-day, families of the same name being found in Giles and other counties of the State.

‡ It is held by a reliable authority already cited—General John Cochrane, President of the New York State Society of the Cincinnati—that a State Society of the Cincinnati *cannot* be dissolved. By the original "Institution" it was "to endure as long as we shall endure" and "is to be perpetuated in our descendants."

What became of its original fund, which, as has been already shown, the State Legislature refused to take charge of on account of the jealousy of, and opposition to, the Society as a military Order with rules of primogeniture?

Had it formally terminated its organization—supposing such action practicable—there would certainly exist some report or record of its formal dissolution. The presumption is that its members succumbed for the time being to the inevitable, from the fact of their scattered residences and difficulty of meeting, as well as to the public hostility alluded to. That the former reasons were not slight at any time is seen from the recorded fact by the Secretary that the President of the Society resided "near two hundred miles from a sea-port town or post-office, so that letters for him had better be sent here.*"

There is doubtless much of both interest and value regarding the Society lying hidden in the archives of the other State Societies, and which it is hoped some diligent seeker may yet enable to see the light of day in the early future.

In the Washington correspondence in the State Department at Washington, and before alluded to, many valuable records regarding the North Carolina regiments exist, and it is possible some additional light might be gained from this source of events just subsequent to the Revolution. †

---

* Letter of Rev. Adam Boyd, Secretary of the North Carolina Society, to General Knox, Secretary-General, dated Wilmington, December 29, 1783. See pages 90, 91.

† List of officers of the First North Carolina Continental battalion from its first establishment, 1775-78; list of officers taken into the First battalion to

A distinguished authority* has reported that all the rolls and records of the North Carolina regiments in the Revolution were hopelessly lost. Yet here we find some very valuable lists in the possession still of the National Government; copies of the rolls of officers of ten other of the State line regiments are in possession of the Missouri Society of Sons of the Revolution,† and it is quite possible still others may yet with diligent research be discovered.

It was stated in January, 1894, that "there were then living in the State lineal descendants of the original sixty-one members and of other Continental officers who are entitled to membership, and it is the patriotic duty of these men to assert their hereditary claims." ‡

And in such case, why should not the North Carolina Cincinnati Society claim its legitimate heritage of restored membership in the General body, and with those other State Societies already there, revive and restore the prestige of the patriotic men of the Revolution in the "old North State"? The descendants of those who fought and suffered in field or camp, during that eventful era in the history of our country, from Stony Point and Germantown to Eutaw

---

complete it, 1777–78; list of officers of the Second North Carolina battalion since 1777; list of officers of the late war, who continued to the end thereof, or were deranged by act of Congress; list of officers of Continental brigade of Brigadier-General Jethro Sumner, 1782, etc. See "Washington Correspondence," Book 115, pp. 142½–143.

* Hon. Walter Clark, Justice of the Supreme Court of North Carolina.

† See also Appendix A, Schenck's "North Carolina, 1780–81," Raleigh, North Carolina, 1889.

‡ "The North Carolina Society of the Cincinnati," by E. G. Daves, *North Carolina University Magazine*, January, 1894.

and Augusta, should be and certainly are worthy of their descent. It needs but a determined energy, with a firm faith in their cause, as had their ancestors before them, and an earnest endeavor of compliance with the requirements of the General Society,* which should not be difficult of attainment on their part, to meet with that honorable recognition which is their just due.

That such success may speedily be the reward of these efforts, is the earnest hope of the writer of these pages.

---

* See Proceedings of General Society of Cincinnati, Boston, Massachusetts, 1872, and Charleston, South Carolina, 1881, in case of application for readmission by Rhode Island State Society.

www.ingramcontent.com/pod-product-compliance
Lightning Source LLC
Chambersburg PA
CBHW021939160426
43195CB00011B/1153